Charlotte Henry is a journalist and broadcaster. She has contributed both freelance and on the staff for a variety of major publications. These include *City AM*, the *Independent on Sunday*, CapX, *Computer Business Review*, the Mac Observer, *The Times* Red Box and the *Times Literary Supplement*.

At all these publications and platforms, she has worked to highlight and explain the collision between technology, politics and the media.

Charlotte has appeared as a pundit on broadcast media, discussing key breaking stories on Sky News, BBC News and a range of regional and national radio stations, as well as doing newspaper reviews.

She has also worked on a variety of political campaigns, advising on digital communication. Charlotte has twice been a candidate herself, running unsuccessfully for the London Assembly and as a local councillor for the Liberal Democrats. Prior to that, she held senior roles in the party's youth wing.

Charlotte grew up in north London, where she still lives. In her spare time, she is a long-suffering fan of Tottenham Hotspur and a lover of rock, dance and heavy metal music. She is also battling (unsuccessfully) an addiction to crime novels. This is Charlotte's first book.

Not Buying It

Not Buying It

Charlotte Henry

unbound

This edition first published in 2019

Unbound
6th Floor Mutual House, 70 Conduit Street, London W1S 2GF
www.unbound.com
All rights reserved

All references to websites were correct at the time of writing.

ISBN (eBook): 978-1-91261-893-4
ISBN (Paperback): 978-1-91261-892-7

Cover design by Mecob

Printed and bound in Great Britain by Clays Ltd, Elcograf S.p.A.

FSC
www.fsc.org

MIX
Paper from
responsible sources
FSC® C018072

Contents

PART IV.
HOW DO WE FIX THIS?

Super Patrons

Luke Akehurst
Steve Andresier
Kate Andrews
Adam Banks
Francesca Barnes
Michael Benson
Emma Burnell
Darren Butler
Tom Cage
Alex Charles
Malcolm Clark
Andy Cohen
Steve Comer
Adam Conn
Vicky Coral
Scott Davies
Dan Davis
Bobby Dean
DG
Kevin Donnellon
Katie Fearn

Barry Ferris
Jonathan Fineberg
Jo and Jeremy Foster
Oli Foster
Daniel Franklin
Andrew Garber
Jacqueline and Gerald Garber
Keith Garber
Steven Garber
Daniele Gibney
Daniel Grabiner
John Grant
Andrew Green
Annabel Green
Daniel Green
David Green
Richard Hanen
Nick 'Herman' Haringman
Jonathan Harrisberg
Daniel Heller
Jan Henry
Sue and Paul Henry
Sarah Henry
Ian Hodge
Amy Hoffbrand
Geoff Hoffman
Marshall Hoffman
Michael Hoffman
Stephen Hoffman
Janice Holve
Bill Horton
Mark Howard
Paula Howard

Lauren Ingram
Anna Isaacs
Bernard Kelly
Cait Kidd
Dan Kieran
Judy Knox
Kirstie Kwan
Pierre L'Allier
Ian Langdon
Shane le Prevost
Joel Levitt
Gordon Lishman
Jacob Livingston
Helen Maggs
Mala Mahadevan
Robbi Malandreniotis
Margaret Marsh
Simon McGrath
Robin Meltzer
David Michael
Carl Minns
Erin Mitchell
John Mitchinson
Gaby Morris
Jeremy Nathan
Jeremy Newmark
Niels Aagaard Nielsen
Alexander Nirenberg
Wystan Palm
Andrew Parsons
Jenny and Keith Pearlman
George Pitcher
Justin Pollard

Thais Portilho
Sharon Portner
Rebecca Quick
Jessica Redhead
Chris Richards
Esther Rinkoff
Eleanor Rose
Margaret Rose
Dan Rosenberg
Gemma and James Rosenfeld
Nicola Rosenfeld
Nina Sandler
Richard Sarsby
Philip Saven
Matthew Searle
Emma Shall Elani
Neil Sherlock
Daniel Simons
Daniel Sonabend
Adam Spensley
Ross Stalker
Cathryn Steele
Mark Thompson
Anthony J. Triano
Albert Wallace
Daniel Waterman
Lois Winter
Greg Woodcock
Hilda Worth

Introduction

The year is 2019, and falsehood and conspiracy have become prominent parts of political discourse around the globe, used by some of the most powerful people in the world to win elections, maintain support from their political bases and destroy their rivals. At the same time, these politicians are branding mainstream media outlets as fake news in an attempt to discredit those who legitimately seek to hold them to account.

Meanwhile, the media itself regularly accuses politicians, and even some other media outlets, of spreading fake news – of lying. All too often, they have good reason for doing so. This is an age in which the truth no longer seems to be sacred. Facts do not matter.

Indeed, Donald Trump, who at the time of writing this book is the president of the United States no less, happily dismisses some of the world's leading media institutions such as CNN and the *New York Times* as 'failing' and 'fake news'. We normally see this when they seek answers to difficult questions about his conduct and policies or simply publish something that he does not like.

For example, in March 2019 Trump took to the airwaves and

Twitter claiming 'complete exoneration' by Special Counsel Robert Mueller's investigation into his campaign.[1] The report did conclude that Trump 'did not conspire' with Russia. However, it 'did not draw a conclusion' on whether there had been any obstruction of justice. Most importantly, a summary sent to Congress by Mueller explicitly said that 'while this report does not conclude that the President committed a crime, it also does not exonerate him.'[2]

In the UK, the 2016 Brexit referendum campaign was tainted by lies and misinformation, some of it infamously painted on the side of a bus. So toxic was the atmosphere that Labour MP Jo Cox was attacked and killed by a far-right thug just days before the vote. The discourse in the years following the poll has not improved much. The negotiation period has been tense and some of the language used against Prime Minister Theresa May utterly vicious and often sexist. One of the MPs in May's own Conservative Party even told a reporter that the prime minister should 'bring her own noose' to a party meeting.

Both sides of the divide in British politics threw out claim and counterclaim, making it almost impossible for members of the general public to decipher what was actually going on. The result was close and divisive tensions remained long after the votes were counted. If anything, they increased, not dissipated, as the painful negotiation process progressed.

Technology inevitably sits at the heart of this story. Information and misinformation are spread with such ease now that lies can take hold in the blink of an eye. The social element of new communications technology means that these lies are so

1. https://www.bbc.co.uk/news/av/world-us-canada-47687956/mueller-report-a-complete-exoneration-donald-trump
2. https://www.bbc.co.uk/news/world-us-canada-47675576

much easier to believe – after all, it's your 'friend', whether real or digital, who is sharing the information with you.

It may be hard for some people to accept, but most journalists do genuinely go into work with the best of intentions – they want to write good, accurate stories that inform, entertain and hold powerful people to account. It is fair to say that, similarly, most politicians go into public service wanting to improve the lives of their constituents. The problem is that a variety of scandals means that far too many now profoundly doubt this.

As we shall see, fake news is not a new phenomenon, but it is clear that something has changed. This book seeks to understand how this has come to pass and to offer some potential ways of fixing the problem. It is based on my own experience working in the media and politics, as well as a range of exclusive interviews with experts working in the media, politics and academia.

The truth is still present in public discourse. We're just not buying it any more.

PART I

What is fake news?

1

Defining the problem

Somewhat typically for the age in which this book is being written, the terms *fake news* and *post-truth* have themselves become distorted, weaponised by some in politics, business and even the media itself to dismiss stories and accusations they do not like. Doing so has proved highly effective. To have any chance of understanding the issue of fake news, let alone tackling it, we must be very clear about what is being discussed.

First, though, it is important to be clear on what fake news is not. It is not information that someone simply dislikes or disagrees with, nor is it articles that contain unintentional and genuine errors from publishers acting in good faith. Such journalism might be wrong, but it is not fake news in any meaningful sense of the term. As former National Union of Journalists president Tim Dawson told me: 'There have always been instances of journalists getting things wrong, but I don't

3

think there's any crime in that, except that you've got to admit to it and put it right as quickly as you can.'

It is intentionality that separates fake news from wrong news.

The broadcaster Ian Collins has been presenting phone-in radio shows for decades and has what he calls the 'privilege' of speaking to real people every day on his programmes. Part of the burden this privilege brings is having to combat total falsehoods put forward by callers live on air. He is therefore better placed than many to understand fake news. 'To me, fake news would be when you've picked an agenda or a view and you've set out deliberately to misinform to gain political advantage,' he says.

Likewise, Professor Charlie Beckett, a long-time filmmaker for the BBC, ITV and Channel 4 who is now an academic working at the London School of Economics' (LSE) POLIS media think tank, told me: 'There's the obvious false, fake hoax news, produced deliberately by commercial people, which is completely false. They know it's false and they're just making money out of it.'

He explains that in addition to this relatively straightforward type of fake news, 'there's kind of politically misrepresentational fake news, where again people know that it's not the whole truth but they're trying to make a political point, they're trying to distort a debate', once again indicating the importance of intent in this discussion.

Beckett says that the issue 'goes right across to people calling something fake news because they disagree with it'. However, he says that intent is important because 'if you do something deliberately it's then also about the accountability of that. So again, if you create something that spreads false information anonymously it's both technically, physically, ethically very different to hold that accountable in any way.'

To take these experts' understanding and experience of the issue and turn it into a broader definition: fake news is deliberately sharing information, despite knowing or suspecting it to be false, for profit and/or political motive. It is content presented as actual news, as 100 per cent fact, but published deliberately by someone who ultimately knows that it is false, or at the very least is unconcerned that it might be.

The Computational Propaganda Project at Oxford University uses the phrase *junk news*. They believe it 'more accurately defines the wide range of bad information that spreads on social media through the powerful algorithms of companies such as Google, Facebook and Twitter'. One of the researchers in that programme, Oxford academic Samantha Bradshaw, explained to me: 'When we were thinking of that definition, we really wanted to avoid the term *fake* because it carries the connotation of something being false or inaccurate or wrong, and it's really hard to determine what someone would see as true because everyone's truth is somewhat objective.'

Bradshaw goes into further detail: 'There are facts and there are things that are true, but people's interpretations of some things, especially partisan ideas in a democracy, can be quite different, and so we use the term *junk news* because we wanted to try and capture content that's bad, it's junk. It's like your junk mail in your inbox.' It is a whole host of information, from phishing attacks to distracting spam, that prevents people from being able to make informed political decisions.

Bradshaw says that while it is likely that 'fake and inaccurate information falls under our category', their term is broader.

While I use the more common phrase *fake news* in this book, in many ways *junk news* is a very good description of the type of material being discussed, and we will cover much that the Oxford University researchers would classify in that way.

Whatever phrase one chooses to use, the issue has shot to the top of the media and political agenda thanks to Donald Trump's shock ascent to the US presidency and the vote for Britain to leave the EU. However, it is far from a new issue, and it goes beyond a few dislikeable figures or controversial issues. Dawson says that there have been 'instances of bona fide made-up, fake news going back, we know, into medieval times'. For example: 'Jews drinking the blood of babies... It didn't happen, but it was widely believed all over Europe.'

Indeed so. A white paper[1] produced by the Computational Propaganda Project also noted that 'the spread of junk news is not a new phenomenon: tabloidization, false content, conspiracy theories and political propaganda all have histories'. From the most serious instances of antisemitism and Holocaust denial to the more easily dismissed tales around water fluoridation, humans transforming into lizards and potential football transfers, falsehood and conspiracy theories have always existed.

The history of these phenomena includes the infamous example of a story published four days prior to the 1924 general election by the *Daily Mail*. The story claimed that the newspaper had a letter proving the Bolshevik regime was, to all intents and purposes, controlling Ramsay MacDonald's Labour government. The newspaper splashed on the headline 'Civil War Plot by Socialists' Masters' and published a list of instructions supposedly given by the Kremlin to the MacDonald government. The story was, of course, nonsense, based on wildly inaccurate information. As Victor Sebestyen

1. https://kf-site-production.s3.amazonaws.com/media_elements/files/000/000/142/original/Topos_KF_White-Paper_Howard_V1_ado.pdf

noted in the *British Journalism Review*: 'If the *Mail* had carried out even cursory checks it might have discovered that its great revelation was based on a forgery.'[2]

Is this fake news or just bad journalism? While one could legitimately argue the latter – after all, many a journalist has fallen foul of bad source material – there is enough intent, or at least knowing negligence, here to meet the definition of fake news. The story was based on false information handed to the journalists, but there can be little doubt that the *Mail* was happy to run that particular story with very few, if any, checks on its validity, simply because it fitted with the paper's political agenda.

A rather more clear-cut example of modern fake news is a story that claimed Pope Francis had endorsed Donald Trump for the presidency of the United States.[3] The story was viewed millions of times online, generating significant income for the publisher. The pope, of course, had not endorsed Donald Trump. Nor had he endorsed anyone else to be the forty-fifth US president. Indeed, no pope has ever endorsed a candidate for the US presidency. The story was just that – a story. A piece of fiction. It was a total falsehood made up to generate clicks, and advertising revenue, for the publisher.

If fake news has been around for decades, centuries even, what has propelled this material to such prominence in recent times? What has changed to make this such a cause for concern? Beckett, for one, is in little doubt. 'It's mainly the internet,' he says. While 'we can generalise about traits,' he says, 'that doesn't mean all people, all the time, are victims to this. But I think definitely the internet has amplified it.'

2. Victor Sebestyen, 'Book Review: Maybe We Like Lies', *British Journalism Review*, 28 (3) (2017).
3. http://www.factcheck.org/2016/10/did-the-pope-endorse-trump/

There have, of course, been falsehood and conspiracy on the web since its dawn. However, the issue has now clearly gone far beyond some standalone stories on largely unread websites in the dusty bowels of the internet or slightly odd characters phoning up late-night talk radio programmes citing such pages as evidence. We will look at this in more depth shortly, but suffice to say for now that thanks to social media, false information can today be shared with absolute ease, making it far more likely that these stories will find their way into the mainstream.

This is not just a Western problem either. Kenya's 2017 general election was thrown into chaos by fake news and the mistrust it sowed amongst the general population. A poll found that a staggering 90 per cent of Kenyans had encountered fake news in the run-up to the hotly contested vote. In this tinderbox atmosphere, an election official who was in charge of the country's electronic voting system was brutally murdered.[4]

The country was susceptible to fake news due to high levels of internet penetration and a collapse in trust for institutions after repeated episodes of violence at previous elections. In violence between different ethnic groups that took place in 2007 and 2008, over 1,000 people died. Furthermore, the country's press had been repressed during the effective dictatorship of Daniel arap Moi, which lasted from 1978 until 2002, meaning that rumour had become an essential channel for disseminating truth and information in the country.

While it is good that so many Kenyans were able to identify fake news, that survey certainly indicates there is a serious issue.

The consequences have been less violent and extreme, but Israel has a growing fake news problem too, prompted by a

---

4. https://www.geopoll.com/blog/fake-news-in-kenyas-2017-general-election-widespread-survey-report/

tech-savvy population and a partisan media ecosystem. Given Israel is the region's only democracy, with enemies on all sides, the stakes of elections are particularly high. In Prime Minister Benjamin Netanyahu, the country also has a political leader who sees the media as the enemy, another crucial element in the spread of fake news.

For example, in March 2018, Netanyahu posted a graphic on his Facebook page that branded various outlets as fake news and specifically attacked Israeli journalist Moshe Nussbaum.[5] Netanyahu's close ally and friend President Trump must have watched on, very proud.

Until those of us in the UK, the US and elsewhere are as savvy as the 90 per cent of Kenyans who could identify the fake news, we should be worried that democracy can be rocked by such material. Furthermore, its prominence in countries around the world, combined with a number of political and social developments, means that we have seen the dawning of an era in which truth has become, if not immaterial, somewhat subjective – the post-truth era.

THE POST-TRUTH ERA

The *Oxford English Dictionary*, which named *post-truth* as its 2016 word of the year, defines the term as an adjective 'relating to or denoting circumstances in which objective facts are less influential in shaping public opinion than appeals to emotion and personal belief'.

This is then an era in which emotion has more prominence than expertise, feelings hold more weight than fact and conspiracy theories can run riot.

Trust in major institutions has all but collapsed, meaning that

---

5. https://www.jpost.com/Israel-News/Benjamin-Netanyahu/Netanyahu-dubs-all-major-Israeli-media-outlets-Fake-News-547165

what they say can be easily dismissed, and perfectly legitimate claims can be rubbished simply on the basis of who is making them. Critical thinking and the ability to question those in power are, of course, essential to a thriving, tolerant liberal democracy. Just because someone in a position of power says something does not mean the general citizenry should believe it. Indeed, the institutions themselves have done much to breed the mistrust now directed towards them.

However, the post-truth era has gone far beyond robust public debate and scepticism and turned into something far more counterproductive and sinister. There is a mood of sneering cynicism in which nothing is to be trusted or believed and a sense prevails that almost all public figures have an ulterior motive, separate from 'people like me'.

Presenting the facts that disprove the lies and conspiracies does not work any more. Such is the level of suspicion that the truth is simply not believed by enough people. All too often, fake news is believed instead.

The BBC's head of live political programmes, Rob Burley, is acutely aware of the issue. He says that he and his colleagues are 'operating in an environment where some people are less trusting of us and they don't know how to distinguish between trustworthy and untrustworthy news sources'.

He points out that outlets with far less robust reporting structures mislead the public by telling them it is the BBC that is untrustworthy and biased. In the current age, far too many people believe that. 'They see that someone is on a programme that they don't like and they think that's evidence of our bias,' says Burley. 'If it is someone they like, they're "on the programme", if it's someone they don't like, they are being "given a platform", and that's the language they use. So they see a line-up of people, and if it includes somebody, a few people they don't like, irrespective of the balance of the programme, they will regard that as being biased.'

In such an environment, those with a public voice begin pandering, deciding that if they can't beat them, they may as well join the digital mob. It is a vicious cycle – these voices then push populist rhetoric and degrade the discourse even further.

We cannot ignore that it is also to the benefit of mainstream outlets that the concern about post-truth thinking is a prominent issue. Beckett says that 'in a way, mainstream media loves fake news because it makes mainstream news look better. "We're not fake, trust us." And the American mainstream media did that especially, and they got massive boosts in their subscriptions, in their ratings, all that sort of stuff.' At a time of financial turmoil for many outlets, painting themselves as the 'good guys' has major strategic benefits.

As Beckett notes, outlets like the *New York Times* and *Washington Post* have, somewhat ironically, benefited from the post-truth era, enjoying soaring subscription levels. The *New York Times* reported that in the last quarter of 2017 alone, it added a net total of 157,000 digital-only subscribers to reach a total of 2.6 million digital-only subscriptions at that time (this includes subscriptions to news, cooking and crossword products).[6] It ended 2018 with 4.3 million total subscribers, 80 per cent of which were digital.[7] The *Washington Post*, meanwhile, proudly revealed in September 2017 that it had hit 1 million paid digital-only subscribers. Serious numbers in anyone's book.

6. https://www.nytimes.com/2018/02/08/business/new-york-times-company-earnings.html
7. https://www.marketwatch.com/story/new-york-times-subscriber-numbers-are-skyrocketing-in-the-trump-age-2019-02-06

Indeed, in February 2017 the *Washington Post* changed the slogan on its masthead to 'democracy dies in darkness'. They insisted that this was not specifically aimed at President Trump and his attacks on the press. However, it is a perfect example of how the establishment press have tried to tap into this moment, to say that as exciting as new outlets can be, it is those with the long history of reporting that the public should trust.

Similarly, in 2018 the *Economist* ran an advertising campaign self-confidently declaring that 'the world needs another *Economist* reader'.

These outlets are without doubt doing worthy work. However, Beckett warns that we must not conflate something being serious and long with it being correct and true. 'I think there is a danger that the truth is synonymous with serious, and that's not true,' he says. 'The truth in people's lives can be emotional, it can be contradictory, it can be about their identity or their imagined identity.'

In a tumultuous era, media companies are obviously having to react to reflect these changes, expectations and contradictions in their audiences. Beckett picks out BuzzFeed as a 'very emblematic company really in a post-truth world. They recognise that people's lives are full of cats and personal listicles about penises and things, but people are also interested, for similar reasons actually, in investigations.'

He also cites the development of *Teen Vogue*, praising them for the way they cover a wide range of subjects, the somewhat silly and the serious. 'Real people are interested in acne, boyfriends and Syria. They recognise that teenage girls encompass all these different things,' he said.

Despite all this, some people, such as the conservative philosopher and writer Sir Roger Scruton, dispute the existence of post-truth culture at all. Writing in the *Spectator* magazine in

June 2017, he said: 'For as long as there have been politicians, they have lied, fabricated and deceived.'[8]

He argues that 'politics is an opinion-forming and opinion-manipulating art. However much people can be influenced by slick advertising, mendacious promises and intoxicating slogans, they are influenced by these things only because the idea of truth lurks somewhere in the background of their consciousness.'

It should be noted that even Scruton, despite his scepticism towards the concept, acknowledges that in his opinion 'the beginning of post-truth culture' was when 'the polytechnic left' began to contend 'that ideas, beliefs and arguments are not to be judged in terms of their truth but in terms of the "class", "hegemony" or "power structure" that speaks through them'.

Somewhat ironically, Scruton himself came to argue that he had fallen victim to what he considered to be politically motivated journalism, which comes rather close to our definition of fake news. In April 2019, he unceremoniously lost his role leading a government architectural commission following a controversial interview with the *New Statesman*. Scruton called on the magazine to publish the recordings, and it subsequently published a transcript of his discussion with its deputy editor.[9]

Cas Mudde, an associate professor in the School of Public and International Affairs at the University of Georgia, also dismissed the significance of the problem in a piece for the *Guardian*. He cites research finding that 'the vast majority of people do not consume fake news, and of the minority that does, the vast majority consume much more real news too. As

8. https://www.spectator.co.uk/2017/06/post-truth-its-pure-nonsense/
9. https://www.spectator.co.uk/2019/04/roger-scruton-should-i-forgive-the-journalist-who-got-me-fired/

far as fake news does play a role, it is in providing legitimacy and support to long-held views by a relatively small group of intense, far right partisans.'[10]

He argues that the so-called 'fake news epidemic' is 'exaggerated' and calls on the media to improve their work instead. He concludes that 'the biggest obstacle to having an informed electorate isn't fake news but, rather, the ever more commercial, profit-seeking media seeking clicks and eyeballs at the expense of nuance, depth and on-the-ground reporting.'

Mudde is making an important point about the strain on resources in journalism and on the disruption the internet has caused to the media's business model. There can be little doubt that the media 'seeking clicks and eyeballs' has led to a plethora of nonsense so-called content.

However, I profoundly disagree with those who try to dismiss the issues of fake news and post-truth. They may write on the subject more eloquently than most, but Scruton and Mudde too readily overlook the fact that something significant has changed in terms of scale and consequence.

For one thing, politics in the post-truth era has been turned upside down. Experience and expertise are mistrusted and consistently lying actually makes people think the likes of Donald Trump are more authentic, not less. The irony of such a situation would be funny were it not so destructive, totally warping political campaigning and debates.

This was seen when Hillary Rodham Clinton was running against Trump in the 2016 US presidential election. Arguably the most qualified candidate ever to run for President, having served as First Lady, Senator and Secretary of State, her enemies stooped to ever-deeper lows to try and undermine her.

10. https://www.theguardian.com/commentisfree/2018/feb/07/hysteria-fake-news-epidemic-distraction

Rumours abounded that Clinton was suffering from serious illness after she became unwell on a couple of occasions during the gruelling campaign. This included fainting at a 9/11 memorial just two months before polling day, which sparked the rumour that she had suffered an epileptic fit.

To prove their point, various outlets replayed, in ever slower motion, a clip of Clinton fainting as she was led to a van by her staff. As any football fan who has ever shouted at television replays of their team's star player being tackled in the penalty area can attest, the more you watch something in slow motion, the more like foul play it looks. So it was here.

Crucially, potently, the falsehood in this case was based on something true. Clinton was ill. She was recovering from a serious concussion, which she had revealed. She had also come down with pneumonia on the campaign trail. These were both conditions that were in the public domain, and her fainting was nothing more sinister than that. However, the collision of fact, fiction and long-term lack of trust in Clinton, brought together courtesy of the internet's conspiracy machine, was devastating – a near-perfect microcosm of the post-truth era.

Not only was it politically damaging to Clinton but it meant that proper debate on substantive issues was replaced with bogus discussions about Clinton's health. The voting public did not go to the ballot box better informed about the people who might be their next president as a result of this coverage.

In a major post-election interview in the *Sunday Times Magazine*, it became clear that Clinton still finds what happened to her campaign, the total collapse in truth, hard to wrap her head around. Discussing another lie, this time one in which she was alleged to be running a child-trafficking ring, she asked the interviewer: 'Do they despise me and my politics so much that they are willing to believe the most horrible lie?'

'How, in democracies like ours, [can] people believe

nonsense and lies on the side of buses about how much money the UK government paid to the EU?' she wondered.

Clinton's despairing questions reveal the entwined relationship between fake news and the post-truth era. You cannot have one without the other – each needs the other to exist and thrive. Without the circumstances of the post-truth era, fake news would not be able to spread with such force. If there were no fake news, there would be much less for those with a post-truth mindset to grasp on to.

For many, the US presidential election in 2016 was the high-water mark of the post-truth era, in which a variety of key factors – the power of social media, an alleged Russian disruption campaign, mistrust of Hillary Clinton and an opponent with the loosest relationship with the truth – collided to create a perfect storm.

There is no doubt that it is an important case study and one that must be looked at in depth, if for no other reason than to help us as citizens understand how democracy can be subverted by untruths, so that we can try to prevent it happening again. However, there is also the risk of focussing solely on a single – admittedly highly compelling – campaign and missing the wood for the trees.

A rejection of the truth has wider consequences, and not just for high-powered people in media and politics. The spread of fake news has even resulted in risk to innocent people's lives, violence and deaths.

A MATTER OF LIFE AND DEATH?

In times of economic uncertainty, during which wars and suffering feature on an almost nightly basis on the news, it is easy to dismiss the issue of fake news as esoteric and irrelevant. With so many other things going on in the world, journalists spending time talking about themselves and their industry seems a luxury at best, a self-aggrandising indulgence at worst.

We cannot ignore it, though, because fake news has morphed into a different and more powerful beast. The serious real-world consequences these changes have brought about mean that fake news cannot simply be dismissed as the navel-gazing concern of middle-class journalists, academics and technologists. It has had a genuine effect on our politics, media and civil society at large and will continue to do so unless we properly understand it and seek to tackle it.

As a whole, society is becoming divided on the back of the mistrust sown by fake news stories. Think of the conspiracy, discussed further in a later chapter on Fox News, that surrounded the death of a man called Seth Rich. He used to work for the Democratic Party and was murdered in Washington, DC. Fox's prime-time presenter Sean Hannity, with very little evidence, repeatedly claimed that Rich had met with representatives of the whistleblowing website Wikileaks and even hinted he might have been killed to assist the Clinton campaign. He backed off pushing the conspiracy only when Fox News retracted the article it published online that made the claim.

Never mind the political consequences, the hurt caused by such a conspiracy must have been excruciating for Rich's bereaved family. Making sure others do not have to go through that is reason enough to tackle the problem of fake news. However, fake news doesn't just speak ill of the dead – it puts the living at risk.

In December 2016 an armed 35-year-old man entered the Comet Ping Pong restaurant in Washington, DC, declaring that he was investigating a conspiracy that Hillary Clinton was running a paedophile ring from the restaurant's basement. The attacker, Edgar Maddison Welch, pointed an assault rifle at an employee of the restaurant, who was quickly able to flee and call police. Customers all say he walked past them with a shotgun – the police found two weapons in the restaurant and another in Welch's car.[11]

This bizarre story Welch claimed to be investigating had started after the pizzeria's name appeared numerous times in emails stolen from Hillary Clinton's campaign chief, John Podesta.[12] As ever, the explanation is a pretty simple one – the pizzeria was near the Clinton team's DC office and the staff regularly ordered food from it during the long days of the campaign. The hacked emails were posted on Wikileaks and seized upon by so-called citizen investigators operating on the online message board 4chan before being picked up by Alex Jones, the man behind the Infowars website, who brought the conspiracy to his huge audience.[13]

Jones eventually apologised for his role in spreading the conspiracy, but the damage had long been done. Whilst the Comet Ping Pong incident thankfully passed without any injuries, the consequences of this fake news could quite literally have been fatal. Following the incident, the restaurant's owner James Alefantis told CNN that what had happened at his establishment 'demonstrates that promoting false and reckless conspiracy theories comes with consequences. I hope that those involved in fanning these flames will take a moment to contemplate what happened here today, and stop promoting these falsehoods right away.'[14]

11. https://edition.cnn.com/2016/12/04/politics/gun-incident-fake-news/index.html
12. https://www.theguardian.com/us-news/2016/dec/05/gunman-detained-at-comet-pizza-restaurant-was-self-investigating-fake-news-reports
13. https://gizmodo.com/pizzagate-shooter-pleads-guilty-as-online-conspiracy-th-1793614716
14. https://money.cnn.com/2016/12/05/media/fake-news-real-violence-pizzagate/index.html

In the UK, the far-left website The Canary gained huge amounts of traction supporting Jeremy Corbyn and his leadership of the Labour Party. Like Infowars, it spread conspiracy theories that eventually pervaded the mainstream. And as with Infowars, those theories ultimately put people's lives at risk.

The Canary's conspiracy revolved around a PR firm called Portland Communications. Reporter Marie Le Conte detailed its rise, and the consequences, in a feature for BuzzFeed News in August 2016. 'It started on 28 June with a piece entitled "The truth behind the Labour coup, when it really began and who manufactured it", written by Steve Topple,' Le Conte reported. 'According to the piece, the Labour frontbench resignations and ensuing rebellion among the parliamentary Labour Party against Jeremy Corbyn were masterminded by PR firm Portland.'

The firm, it was alleged, was staffed by those who had worked in the Labour Party under Tony Blair, the political enemy of Corbyn and his supporters. They had apparently orchestrated a succession of resignations from Corbyn's shadow ministerial team to try to bring down his then-ailing leadership. Crucially, the conspiracy theory grew so prominent online that it made it onto major Sunday morning political television courtesy of Len McCluskey, leader of Britain's largest trade union, Unite, who made the claims on the BBC's *Andrew Marr Show*.

Not long after that, Kevin McKeever, a Labour activist who had not supported Jeremy Corbyn and who was at the time a partner at Portland, received a death threat at his office. The note warned him that 'your blood is the price of your treachery' and that he should 'prepare to be coxed [*sic*]', a grotesque reference to the murder of Labour MP Jo Cox, who had been killed by a far-right terrorist just days earlier.

In June 2018, a man arrived at a news room of the *Capital Gazette* in Annapolis, Maryland, USA, and shot and killed five people there – four of whom were journalists, the other a young sales assistant. The man who carried out the shooting, Jarrod Ramos, had a long-standing feud with the paper, having unsuccessfully tried to sue it for defamation some years earlier.

However, many also saw a connection between the incident and the growing anti-media sentiment led by US president Donald Trump and the hyperpartisan sites and commentators that support him. Just days before the shooting, Milo Yiannopoulos, a controversial right-wing online firebrand and the former tech editor at one such site, Breitbart News, had told a website called the Observer in a text message that he '[couldn't] wait for the vigilante squads to start gunning journalists down on sight'.[15] Following the shooting, he claimed he had been joking.

In an editorial in the wake of the attack, the *Baltimore Sun*, whose parent company owned the *Capital Gazette*, wrote a damning indictment of both US gun laws and the anti-media sentiment that was building up in the country courtesy of fake news sites.

The powerful piece noted the politically divided time and how many people quickly wondered 'whether the metaphorical war on the media had become shockingly literal'. The attack left many reporters with a 'sickening feeling', the newspaper said. 'They couldn't believe something like this had happened, except that they could.'[16]

The terrible incident also brought the US into the ranks

15. http://observer.com/2018/06/milo-yiannopoulos-encourages-vigilantes-start-gunning-journalists-down/
16. http://www.baltimoresun.com/news/opinion/editorial/bs-ed-0629-capital-gazette-shooting-20180628-story.html

of the most dangerous countries for journalists in 2018. The deaths of the four journalists in Annapolis, along with those of two journalists covering Subtropical Storm Alberto in North Carolina in May that year, meant that the number of journalist deaths in the US was mostly only surpassed in warzones.[17]

The polarised, angry language that characterises so much of modern political debate also saw numerous pipe bombs sent to prominent critics of President Trump in October 2018. These included President Trump's predecessor Barack Obama and his opponent Hillary Clinton as well as former vice president Joe Biden and actor Robert De Niro. One was also sent to CNN, a channel regularly criticised by President Trump, resulting in an evacuation of the building in which the station is based. None of the bombs went off, this time, and a suspect was arrested after an intense FBI investigation.[18]

As news of the bombs was emerging and people were, at least in part, increasingly blaming President Trump's incendiary rhetoric for inciting it, he remained unrepentant, tweeting: 'A very big part of the Anger we see today in our society is caused by the purposely false and inaccurate reporting of the Mainstream Media that I refer to as Fake News. It has gotten so bad and hateful that it is beyond description. Mainstream Media must clean up its act, FAST!'[19]

Days later, with the suspect caught, he said that far from toning down his rhetoric, he could 'tone it up'. He even joined in as a small crowd he was addressing chanted 'lock him up' about George Soros, who had also received a bomb in the post, in an echo of chants he used to lead about Hillary Clinton.

17. https://rsf.org/en/news/rsfs-2018-round-deadly-attacks-and-abuses-against-journalists-figures-all-categories
18. https://www.nytimes.com/2018/10/24/nyregion/clinton-obama-explosive-device.html
19. https://twitter.com/realDonaldTrump/status/1055418269270716418

The threats did not end there. In December 2018 CNN staff again found themselves evacuated. Someone had phoned up claiming five devices had been planted in the building. So serious was the threat that even the on-air presenter at the time, Don Lemon, was told to leave, with the channel cutting to a re-run.[20]

It is clear, then, that the issues of fake news and post-truth have gone beyond the esoteric and can in fact result in the most serious of consequences. The critical question we first need to ask was posed by the one-time next president of the United States in that *Sunday Times Magazine* interview: 'How did we let this happen?'[21]

20. https://edition.cnn.com/2018/12/07/media/reliable-sources-12-06-18/index.html
21. Hillary Clinton interview with Christina Lamb in *Sunday Times Magazine*, 8 October 2017.

PART II

How did we get here?

2

Saving Tinkerbell: the engines of belief

'To save Tinkerbell', the *Washington Post*'s esteemed media columnist Margaret Sullivan wrote in March 2017, 'all you had to do was clap your hands and really, really believe in fairies. To send a conspiracy theory on its vicious way around the world, you need to do more than just believe. You need help.'[1]

That help is now present in spades, with a variety of circumstances conspiring to create an ideal environment for fake news to prosper.

This is thanks in no small part to an online infrastructure that spreads deceit and misinformation around the globe quicker than they can be corrected. Spreading bogus information used to take time and effort. Not any more. The internet, and social media in particular, has made publishing and sharing misinformation, disinformation and lies easier than ever before.

We are no longer dependent on the traditional gatekeepers

---

1. https://www.washingtonpost.com/lifestyle/style/pro-trump-media-sets-the-agenda-with-lies-heres-how-traditional-media-can-take-it-back/2017/03/11/4f30f768-050a-11e7-b9fa-ed727b644a0b_story.html

– mainstream media outlets and their editors who commission stories – to be able to publish or access information. Gatekeepers do still exist in the form of Facebook, Google and Twitter, but most people can at least access and use these sites. Having such power concentrated in such a small number of firms is problematic, but it can be argued that it is more democratic than limiting the ability to publish to those working in newspapers, magazines or television.

At its best, social media is connective, informative and fun. However, with the barriers to entry so low, mischief makers have free rein to publish what they want in order to distort, disrupt and bully. These social media platforms have given people almost total latitude to spread the most grotesque lies, and they are now struggling to decide whether they are publishers with editorial control over the content that appears on their websites or neutral platforms that let users post whatever they want.

Given the vast power such firms have, it is unclear if they are even the right people to fix the problem they have helped create. Meanwhile, fake news is having serious real-world consequences.

Theoretically, the ability to publish easily should help counter fake news – the tools are the same for both sides, after all, so publishing the truth should be no more difficult than publishing lies. However, the velocity at which these lies travel means that they are seen by so many people in such a short space of time that they become firmly embedded before any attempt at redress can take place. Day in and day out we see the phrase 'a lie can travel halfway around the world while the truth is still putting on its shoes' (ironically often incorrectly attributed to Mark Twain) come true.[2]

2. https://www.nytimes.com/2017/04/26/books/famous-misquotations.html

That is because the answer to the fake news question does not begin and end with social media, or with technology at all. Political ideology and scandal have also played crucial supporting roles in the spreading of fake news. Discontent with the political class has reached boiling point. Subsequently, those previously on the political fringes have moved front and centre, and politics has become ever more polarised. In parallel, key institutions have been found wanting, unable to respond to the fast-moving circumstances.

As journalism professor Jeff Jarvis correctly noted on his blog: '"Fake news" is merely a symptom of greater social ills. Our real problems: trust and manipulation. Our untrusted – and untrustworthy – institutions are vulnerable to manipulation by a slew of bad guys, from trolls and ideologues to Russians and terrorists, all operating under varying motives but similar methods.'[3]

Either way, in the midst of this perfect storm, the liberal centre of politics has almost totally collapsed. Those on the extreme left and right are gleefully dancing on its remains, supported by websites spreading hyperpartisan, polarising and totally fake information and exploiting the subsequent political tension for eyeballs and profit. Terrified of being swept away, too many in public life seem happy to play along with this dangerous game. Previously mainstream politicians and commentators can be found cashing in on these fraught political times instead of trying to resolve the divisions.

We will certainly look at all these issues. It is impossible to understand the post-truth era, let alone go some way to fixing it, without doing so. However, it is with social media that our discussion must begin. It has changed the media landscape

3. https://medium.com/whither-news/our-problem-isnt-fake-news-our-problems-are-trust-and-manipulation-5bfbcd716440

beyond recognition, as dramatically as Johannes Gutenberg's printing press or John Logie Baird's television did, and it plays a starring role in the story of fake news. It has given Tinkerbell all the help she needs.

BEING SOCIABLE

Services such as Facebook, Twitter, YouTube and Instagram have allowed us all to connect instantly with friends, family and strangers anywhere in the world – sharing our pictures, videos and stories, our loves and hates, hopes and fears. These services have become central to how people socialise, date and reconnect with those they have lost touch with, not to mention how we consume news. They have, however, also provided the technological basis that has allowed the extreme and the false to flourish.

Tim Dawson said that the development of this technology 'means we are now consuming a lot of news through social, much of which isn't professionally mediated. Our whole relationship to the mass media has changed.'

People have shot to fame and entire media outlets have been built on the back of social media due to its ability to quickly and cheaply get content in front of a large number of people. It is this ease of sharing that is so crucial to the dissemination of fake news. The most positive elements of social media have been twisted into a negative – the effort required to spread fake news is minimal, the potential reach enormous.

The services have given social cachet to views disguised as news, true and false information and everything in between. In the same way that we prefer to get hotel or restaurant recommendations from a friend or family member, if someone we know shares a news story, it gives it credence and makes us more likely to believe that item. The original source of the story is less relevant. This extends to social media personalities with whom people feel they have developed a personal relationship, and consequently trust what they say.

What is more, the amount of data social media companies hold on individuals means that political campaigns, or even those just wishing to cause disruption, can target fake news at those likely to be the most receptive. Samantha Bradshaw gave a fairly typical example when interviewed on this: 'When parties are buying ads, they can target black women living in major cities in the US and between the ages of 18 and 24. Send them one version of an ad that would be different from the ad going to white men, 18 to 24, living in Texas, something like that.'

The targeted spreading of fake news is not just about encouraging your own supporters; it can equally be about agitating or demotivating those who back your opponent. Bradshaw explains: 'I think with the 2016 Trump campaign there were ads targeting black women that were talking about how Hillary Clinton was racist and she didn't support certain policies that would benefit black women because black women were more likely to vote Democrat than they were conservative, and so as you start putting those ideas in people, they might not change their mind but they might not go out and vote.'

Much of the conversation around fake news focusses on Facebook. More than any of its rivals, it lies at the heart of the fake news social media ecosystem. Part of this is down to its sheer scale – it is huge, boasting over 2 billion users. As James Ball notes in his book *Post-Truth*, Facebook gets 80 times as many users per day as MailOnline, the biggest news website on the internet, and even greater orders of magnitude more users than the BBC's flagship *News at 10* broadcast or its major US equivalents.[4]

It is not just size that matters here, though. Facebook's very nature leaves it susceptible to fake news. It is based on the

4. James Ball, *Post-Truth* (Biteback, 2017), p. 145.

concept of friends, and as mentioned, we are naturally far more likely to share information given to us by our friends and relatives than by people we may not know on Twitter or other social media sites.

People had hoped that, as well as sharing information amongst people who know each other, services such as Facebook would help bring about a new era of meaningful, intelligent 'citizen journalism' alongside traditional outlets. In a report published by the Columbia Journalism School's Tow Center for Digital Journalism, Emily Bell and Taylor Owen write: 'In encouraging news businesses to make fuller use of Facebook as a distribution outlet, Facebook had in turn opened publishing tools to everyone else too.'[5] What was available only to professionals is now available to amateurs, for good and for ill.

However, Bell and Owen conclude that changes within Facebook had ultimately led to the 'creation of a system that exacerbated the spread of false information during the 2016 election cycle'.

The report notes that, despite the protests of Zuckerberg and other senior figures at his firm, 'Facebook is, without doubt, the largest publishing company in the world with 1.9 billion active users and 2 trillion searchable posts'. (Since their report was written, Facebook went on to break the 2 billion user mark.)

Bell and Owen cite rigorous reporting from BuzzFeed News' Alex Kantrowitz, who wrote one of the first pieces to really look at fake news in depth. Kantrowitz noted that a mere eight days after Barack and Michelle Obama tweeted a picture of themselves with the caption 'Four more years' – which became the most shared tweet ever – Facebook launched its

5. https://www.cjr.org/tow_center_reports/platform-press-how-silicon-valley-reengineered-journalism.php/

'Share' button. This gave users the ability to highlight things to their Facebook friends far more easily than they ever had before, as they already could on Twitter – it brought ease of sharing content to the platform that had the largest audience.

It was a game changer for the spreading of fake news. Friends could now share things with each other in an instant where they had previously needed to copy and paste links. It was also launched on Facebook's mobile app first, often encouraging people to share quickly whilst on the go and provide little context. 'On mobile where typing is more of a pain, a Share button could encourage people to rapidly re-share link after link,' TechCrunch commented at the time of the launch.[6]

Stories that go viral on Facebook can bring in huge amounts of advertising revenue for publishers. This incentivises publishers to post items that are emotive and engaging – perfect for fake news.

Indeed, thanks to the power of social media, one town in the Balkans found itself at the heart of something of a fake-news-inspired digital gold rush. Veles is a small town in Macedonia. There is not much for young people to do there and little opportunity to earn a good income, but some residents discovered they could generate viral fake news over Facebook and reap the rewards from advertising.

One report in *Wired* magazine found an example of an 18-year-old in Veles who earned $16,000 between August and November 2016 from the two pro-Trump websites he ran. This is particularly significant when it is considered that the average monthly wage in Macedonia is $371. The young Macedonian men – and they were mostly young men – behind the fake news sites cared very little about the result of the US election or how their websites might affect the outcome. They

6. https://techcrunch.com/2012/11/14/facebook-mobile-share-button/

just wanted the cash. 'This is the arrhythmic, disturbing heart of the affair,' noted reporter Samanth Subramanian, 'that the internet made it so simple for these young men to finance their material whims and that their actions helped deliver such momentous consequences.'[7]

In the face of huge public criticism following the 2016 US election, Facebook tried to bring in systems to tackle the issue of fake news spreading on its platform. It partnered with trusted outlets like ABC News and the Associated Press as well as fact-checking sites such as Snopes.com and PolitiFact to highlight false stories that were spreading on Facebook and warn people not to share them. Such stories would be marked with a 'disputed flag', telling readers that there could be issues with the content.

The success of this project in reducing the spread of fake news was minimal at best. Shortly after the programme launched, Melissa Zimdars, an assistant professor of communication at Merrimack College, told the *Guardian* that she felt it was 'ultimately kind of a PR move'[8] by Facebook. 'It's cheap to do. It's easy. It doesn't actually require them to do anything,' she added.

While a Facebook spokesman insisted that 'we have seen that the disputed flag does lead to a decrease in traffic and shares', many of the partner organisations also expressed scepticism at the effect of their work. So too did the writers of fake news, with one, Robert Shooltz, who runs the fake news website RealNewsRightNow, insisting that the moves 'had absolutely no effect'. He also claims that his site is satirical, making it even harder to pin down.[9]

7. https://www.wired.com/2017/02/veles-macedonia-fake-news/
8. https://www.theguardian.com/technology/2017/may/16/facebook-fake-news-tools-not-working
9. Ibid.

Furthermore, legitimate local news site the Newport Buzz actually found that when an article (which did contain a legitimate error) on their site was labelled as fake news traffic actually went up, with conservative groups sharing it widely to counter what they thought was an attempt to silence the site. This hints at the culture war that lies at the heart of the post-truth era and will be discussed later in the book.

Facebook is stuck between the proverbial rock and hard place on this issue. It tried bringing in journalists to curate and edit its Trending section, which can send thousands or even millions of readers to a news story, but there were allegations of political bias. The firm then brought in an algorithm for this section, but that actually helped spread fake news and nonsense.

Perhaps it is no surprise then that Facebook seems to be moving away from news, reducing the content in the News Feed published by media, businesses and brands in favour of updates from users' friends and family.[10] It has also removed the Trending section, with the company claiming that it had 'found that over time people found the product to be less and less useful'. A more cynical view is that the tool had come under criticism, not least for suppressing conservative news stories, and so actually added to Facebook's problems in the area of news.[11] Being the world's newsstand ultimately became too big a risk to the firm's reputation.

Most ominously, it is not just humans who are spreading misinformation online. There is the growing phenomenon of bots, particularly on Twitter, automatically sharing false information on certain topics. Bradshaw, whose team is based at the Oxford University Internet Institute, explained to me that 'bots are just

10. https://www.vox.com/2018/1/12/16882536/facebook-news-feed-changes
11. https://www.theverge.com/2018/6/1/17417428/facebook-trending-topics-being-removed

essentially bits of automated code you plug in to an API. You can build a bot to have certain responses to things.'

An API, or Application Programming Interface, is a bit of code that allows websites and apps to be connected to one another. It is the code that allows you to use Facebook to log in to certain other services, for example. In this case, the code that Twitter made publicly available so developers can integrate the service into their apps and websites is used to connect to the automated bots Bradshaw describes.

There is a wide range of different types of bots, and 'some are definitely more sophisticated than others', she says. While some 'will have human-like interactions with people or when it comes to things online', others 'might just retweet or share certain stories that contain certain hashtags'.

Somewhat frighteningly, Bradshaw adds that 'you can link all these different bot accounts together to create a botnet'. This is particularly important in the spread of fake news, as this technology 'might work on amplifying certain stories'. Furthermore, other types of bots focus on trying to gain more followers 'because if they can get real people following them, then when they do send out a message it's like a real person, which means it might have more sway'.

In a large number of cases, it is almost impossible for even the most critical and informed of users to tell if they are interacting with a real account or a fake one, and so, of course, the platforms themselves struggle to do so.

'Everyone's really worried for the future of all these challenges,' said Bradshaw. 'As these technologies get more sophisticated it might be even harder to identify what's real and what's fake. Especially when you can create entirely fake images of people using AI and software and stuff like that.'

The social network companies have become aware of the issues of misleading paid-for advertising and bots. Indeed, when Facebook founder and CEO Mark Zuckerberg appeared for questioning in front of a US congressional committee, this is what he primarily focussed on.

However, the insidious content designed to go viral and be spread by humans, not bots, in order to disrupt politics and disseminate lies is a lot harder for Facebook to deal with. A picture can tell a thousand words, the cliché goes, and visual content in particular has become crucial to spreading fake news on social media. Graphics and pictures, often made into memes – humorous images or videos designed to be shared quickly and widely around the internet – go viral, spreading misinformation in an easily digestible form to potentially millions of people.

When grilling Zuckerberg, Mark Warner, the Democratic politician and vice chair of the Intelligence Committee, highlighted one incident during the 2016 US presidential election campaign. A Russian-run Facebook page called 'Army of Jesus' posted a picture that depicted Hillary Clinton as the Devil, with the caption '"Like" if you want Jesus to win'. This was nothing less than out-and-out disruption in the democratic process, designed to stop people, presumably Christians in this case, voting for Clinton.

Another meme that spread was a video claiming that David Hogg, a survivor of the February 2018 Parkland, Florida, school shooting was a crisis actor, someone paid to portray that they had been caught up in a disaster, and not a genuine victim. At one point, the totally false video making this accusation was the top-trending item on YouTube.[12]

Similarly, doctored images of fellow Parkland survivor Emma Gonzalez ripping up the American Constitution spread

12. https://www.cnet.com/news/florida-shooting-conspiracy-theories-trends-on-youtube-facebook/

around the internet, with millions of people seeing them before it could be pointed out that they were false – the pictures were manipulated versions of shots taken of Gonzalez for *Teen Vogue*, in which she ripped up shooting targets.[13]

Relatives of victims of another horrific mass shooting, in Sandy Hook, suffered similarly. Leonard Pozener, the son of six-year-old victim Noah, found himself having to spend hours every day trying to remove conspiracy theories about the shooting from the web. He took Infowars' Alex Jones to court.[14] He and Noah's mother, Veronique De La Rosa, wrote an open letter to Mark Zuckerberg. They told the Facebook CEO that 'we are unable to properly grieve for our baby or move on with our lives because you, arguably the most powerful man on the planet, have deemed that the attacks on us are immaterial, that providing assistance in removing threats is too cumbersome, and that our lives are less important than providing a safe haven for hate'.[15]

Human beings have done all this, not algorithms. And humans need to fix it.

Back in the UK, the BBC's Rob Burley has found himself on the front line of this digital battle for truth. He chooses to deal with the issue directly, often publicly challenging people making false accusations about the programmes he is involved in. The issue for him is particularly prominent on Twitter, where people often hurl accusations of bias against the BBC's political programming, claiming the decisions of who gets interview slots on the big-ticket programmes as evidence.

Burley uses social media to push back, taking the fight to his

13. https://www.snopes.com/fact-check/emma-gonzalez-ripping-up-constitution/
14. https://www.nytimes.com/2018/08/13/business/media/sandy-hook-conspiracies-leonard-pozner.html
15. https://www.theguardian.com/commentisfree/2018/jul/25/mark-zuckerberg-facebook-sandy-hook-parents-open-letter

critics by taking to Twitter to answer them directly. Despite being a senior figure at the BBC he takes the time to do this because 'if you don't, if you just leave the field, then that's a risky thing because it means there's nobody out there'. If he doesn't counter the conspiracies about his programmes, nobody else will.

Burley's tweets can be witty and cutting as he determinedly takes on the falsehoods his detractors try to spread. He explained that he takes this approach in the hope of changing some people's perceptions of the BBC. His intention is that some people will see the funny replies, see that at least some at the BBC have a sense of humour and think 'actually they've got a point' about some of the more ridiculous accusations thrown their way.

All too often, though, he is fighting a losing battle, as are the many other people trying to correct inaccuracies online. Just as lies help some politicians seem authentic, plenty of people actually see attempts to rebut their claims as further proof that they are right.

INFORMATION OVERLOAD

Have you ever walked into a book shop and suddenly felt overwhelmed, realising that there are just so many topics you know nothing about? Or started reading a quick article on the internet, only to find yourself down a rabbit warren of information, but none the wiser about the topic as you're unable to process it all? That sense is information overload.

We have so much information available to us now, with new information arriving almost constantly; overwhelmed by the sheer scale of the task of processing it all, we have become unable to tell what is fact or fiction.

At any moment, a person can be receiving emails from colleagues and clients, reading WhatsApp messages from friends and family and flicking through the latest snaps on Instagram, whilst Twitter replies and Facebook notifications flood in and breaking news alerts appear in near real time. That's all on a small device held in one individual's hand.

Smartphones have become central to the way many people receive information. While they can perform all manner of complex tasks in an instant, they still cannot differentiate between what is true and false, important and irrelevant. A phone does not know that a rumour your friend shared on WhatsApp is probably less substantiated than something extensively reported by a professional news organisation. But it is all there, on the same platforms on the same devices, and it all looks the same.

As human beings have developed, we have learned to process increasing amounts of information – from the communication methods of early man to the elaborate vocabulary and digital tools we have now. The sum of human knowledge has, of course, increased too. Every era has more information and more ways of communicating that information than the ones preceding it did. That situation has reached new levels in the current era, providing a real sense of information overload.

In the introduction to her 2011 work *Too Much to Know*, the Harvard historian Ann M. Blair says that 'the perception of overload is best explained... not simply as the result of an objective state, but rather as the result of a coincidence of causal factors, including existing tools, cultural or personal expectations, and changes in the quantity or quality of information to be absorbed and managed'.[16]

Indeed, Blair notes that 'the Renaissance experienced information overload on a hitherto unprecedented scale, drawing a parallel with our experience today'.[17]

16. Ann M. Blair, *Too Much to Know* (Yale University Press, 2010), p. 3.

She explains that the ancient Egyptian Ptolemy family sought to catalogue everything written in Greek in the great library at Alexandria to try to organise it for their scholars.[18] It is a noteworthy example that reveals further historical precedent for today's situation. We have always wanted to feel in control of information, but it has never been more difficult.

The LSE's Professor Beckett says that 'we are now in a position where we've got so much information, so many different sources, that I think people are genuinely disorientated and unsure and sceptical about information in general and the news in particular'. He cites Blair's work and reiterates how she 'talks about how in the Middle Ages people felt they were overwhelmed by information and much of it was unreliable and so they created systems to try to process information. One system was called a library. Another system was called an encyclopaedia.'

History can only take us so far, though. We are now dealing with a volume of information at a totally different order of magnitude than in the past. To give some idea of how rapid this change has been, in 2013 leading Norwegian research centre SINTEF revealed that 90 per cent of the data in the world had been created in just the previous two years. That same year, tech giant IBM said that 2.5 quintillion bytes of data were created every day, including data from 'sensors used to gather shopper information, posts to social media sites, digital pictures and videos, purchase transactions and cell phone GPS signals'.

Three years after those reports, human beings were found to be consuming more media than ever before. A 2016 report by Zenith found that people around the globe spent, on average,

17. Ibid., p. 11.
18. Ibid., p. 16.

456.1 minutes of every day consuming media. That's nearly a third of the day, every day, being used to consume media, with a large part of that driven by mobile devices.

Some of this is down to a change of what we mean by media. We now interact with friends and family in the same way we interact with media. So you might share a picture with a family member via Instagram direct messaging – that would constitute media behaviour. Zenith's head of forecasting explained that there had been a shift of 'what used to be non-media activity (talking to friends and family) to media activity (social media)'.[19] (It is also worth noting that the number dropped slightly in 2017, but it still remained remarkably high.)

We can try to use older systems as a good basis for moving forward – for instance, Google essentially acts as the world's online library. However, the sheer scale of information that we are faced with, while wonderful in many ways, is almost impossible to organise and process.

To compound the issue further, more and more of us increasingly do not take in information in its entirety. A 2017 report by the IPA found that 92 per cent of adults in Great Britain were consuming two media or more during the same half an hour at some point during a week, with more than a quarter consuming three or more. The constant distractions on offer make it even harder to decide what is worth believing and what is not.

Instead of reading something in full, we skim through a news story because there's already a pop-up alert demanding you read a newer one; we read a 280-character instant reaction on Twitter instead of waiting to hear something more

19. https://www.recode.net/2017/5/30/15712660/media-consumption-zenith-mobile-internet-tv

thoughtful because it is there and we are impatient to have it right away. It is hard to judge information sceptically when you try to take it in so quickly, and this makes it so much easier to fall for fake news.

Some outlets, such as the *Guardian*, are trying to alter this, offering more in-depth types of journalism such as a weekly 'Long Read' piece. Such works are popular, but publishers cannot entirely ignore what their audience is demanding. 'There's a sort of paradox,' says Beckett, 'that we are getting faster and slower. We want super, super fast, literally a few words, telling us what's going on. A notification that goes *ping, ping, ping*, but at the same time we want to indulge in a three-, four-minute video or a twenty-minute read.'

In the ancient Greek age that Blair refers to, education and knowledge were limited to the elites, meaning only they had to contend with the issue of information overload. This is increasingly no longer the case, particularly in the Western world, as access to the internet and information is becoming ever faster, cheaper and easier. This is now a problem for everyone.

As well as recognising the unprecedented scale of information we are dealing with, we need to understand the cultural issues that fuel our sense of information overload.

Our culture demands that we, as individuals, have ever more information all the time. 'I don't know' is rarely an acceptable answer any more. We know there is so much information available and so have become terrified of missing out on any of it – from news stories to trivia. The trend for newspaper review shows or email newsletters, for instance, promising to give us tomorrow's news today is the perfect demonstration of this mindset – everybody wants to know everything, all the time and often right away.

If FOMO is 'fear of missing out', normally on social

experiences, we live in an age of INFOMO – a fear of missing out on information.

Perhaps this desire to have an answer right away has always been part of human nature, but now we have the technology to make such instant informational gratification possible. The answer to a quiz question is always in the palm of your hand; somebody with a new tale to tell or the new must-have item is just a click away; the latest news or sports highlights and restaurant reviews are instantly available. Author Michael Patrick Lynch calls this 'Google knowing', a phrase he says 'helps describe how we acquire information and knowledge via the testimony machine of the internet'.[20]

We know there is so much information out there, so when you read something in a quick, distracted manner, you can just accept that what you have read is a truth you had not previously been aware of. It seems entirely reasonable that someone knows something you do not. That awareness makes it all too easy to believe that even the most egregious conspiracy theories could be correct.

The need for speed in most forms of journalism exacerbates all these problems. This is particularly true of 24-hour news channels. Indeed, when this style of broadcasting started, the channels were so determined to be first that accuracy was sometimes sacrificed, leading to the jibe 'never wrong for long'. They are the perfect example of INFOMO. Terrified of missing out on something, of a rival having something to say while they are silent, they often bring people on who speculate on situations about which very little is known.

Beckett argues that 'we've actually gone from twenty-four-hour news to two-to-four-hour news'. He says that 'you can

20. Michael Patrick Lynch, *The Internet of Us* (Liveright Publishing, 2016).

see this around major incidents like terrorism. People's understanding of an event is formed within four hours.'

This situation is something broadcaster Ian Collins has to contend with. 'I did have, during one of the terrorist attacks in Europe, I think it was Berlin in the marketplace, there was somebody was emailing who was getting very upset about the fact that we had experts on speculating,' he recalls.

Collins argues that 'speculation is not a bad thing' and that 'it's not a sensationalist approach for journalists to speculate'. He adds that 'to speculate can be intelligent, and it can be healthy and it can be reasonable'. However, he also acknowledges that 'we live in a twenty-four-hour media village now so sometimes you need speculation'.

That is an honest admission. The truth is, though, that as good as presenters like Collins are at drawing out the facts and making it clear what is known and what is speculation, this method of filling airtime ultimately adds more noise than signal. It also risks blurring the lines about what is a fact and what is not for viewers and listeners, making it harder to grasp the reality of a situation. Fake news can spread by feeding off this speculation and uncertainty.

Bots, the automated accounts churning out information that Samantha Bradshaw described, have also contributed to the sense of information overload. If nothing else, they have added to the sheer amount of information we have to wade through to get to any substance. They also consciously ratchet up the volume on certain topics and can spread disinformation and inaccuracies for a variety of ulterior purposes. They add nothing but confusion to many public conversations.

With all this going on, it is no wonder we are struggling to work out what is real and what is not.

PARTISAN NEWS AND PUNCH AND JUDY POLITICS

Essential to the fake news ecosystem are hyperpartisan, ideologically driven websites that build a devoted following via social media. Purporting to be news outlets, they publish information in a highly editorialised and often extreme fashion. Some of these names, such as Breitbart News, have come to be recognised by the general public. Others, such as neo-Nazi site the Daily Stormer, are less generally well known but still attract a huge audience and wield real influence.

The individuals involved at these outlets have also become significant political players, particularly in the US. Most famously, Steve Bannon led the Breitbart organisation for a number of years before being hired by Donald Trump to manage his presidential campaign and then to be his chief strategist in the White House.

But there is also Sebastian Gorka, who was a deputy assistant to Trump largely focussed on the highly sensitive issue of counterterrorism, despite there being serious questions about his level of expertise in the topic.[21] Similarly, Julia Hahn, often described as Bannon's protégée, is a former Breitbart editor who rose through the ranks of the Trump White House communications team.[22]

Alongside Breitbart, conservative outlets such as Infowars distort news in the most extreme way possible. Indeed, Matt Drudge formed a whole site that operates like this, the Drudge Report, and earned huge wealth and influence by putting a conservative and sensationalist spin on headlines. These publications largely hold on to the coattails of the outlet that

21. https://edition.cnn.com/2017/08/18/politics/gorka-credentials/index.html
22. https://www.politico.com/story/2018/06/17/trump-white-house-communications-650394

most typifies this hyperpartisan form of news coverage – Fox News. So great is Fox's influence that the channel and the ecosystem it sits at the heart of must be looked at in more depth, which we will do in a later chapter.

These sites, although ostensibly rivals competing for scoops, eyeballs and advertising revenue, often play off each other, repeating and building on each other's stories, creating an ecosystem in which a certain message is constantly reinforced. With trust in the mainstream media so low, increasing numbers of users do not countenance information they get from other outlets. Some do not even bother to read mainstream publications, giving the more extreme platforms yet further power and influence.

Looking at them, you would be forgiven for thinking there was a parallel universe they were reporting on. For example, Breitbart regularly ran stories attacking former FBI director James Comey and dismissed the potential for Russian meddling in the 2016 presidential election. However, US intelligence agencies do think that Russia was behind a hacking campaign against Hillary Clinton, although President Trump himself was not found guilty of collusion by the Mueller report.[23]

Breitbart sits at the heart of this ecosystem in the US. In a study of 1.25 million stories published online between 1 April 2015 and the US presidential election on 8 November 2016, the *Columbia Journalism Review* found that 'a right-wing media network anchored around Breitbart developed as a distinct and insulated media system, using social media as a backbone to transmit a hyperpartisan perspective to the world'.[24]

However, this parallel universe sometimes crossed over, and

23. https://www.bloomberg.com/news/articles/2019-03-28/russia-urges-u-s-to-publish-mueller-report-on-meddling-in-full
24. https://www.cjr.org/analysis/breitbart-media-trump-harvard-study.php

the journal found that as well as setting the agenda of the conservative media landscape, pro-Trump media 'strongly influenced the broader media agenda'. As they seeped into the mainstream, the rumours and conspiracies published by Breitbart and others had to be debated by politicians and news anchors, giving them some level of validation. People saw credible outlets discussing these stories and decided they must therefore have some truth to them.

In her column referenced earlier, Sullivan cites examples of how news about hacked Hillary Clinton emails spread from 'replies to the WikiLeaks Twitter account, through conservative radio and then Breitbart News, and out into the semi-mainstream – Sean Hannity on Fox News – all within 48 hours' – a breathtakingly short amount of time for such damage to be done in. Another example she gives is the right-wing radio host Mark Levin starting the rumour, without any obvious evidence, that President Barack Obama had ordered that then-candidate Trump be wiretapped. This story 'made its way quickly through the media ecosystem, after Trump saw it, apparently on Breitbart News'.

This ecosystem exists on the far left in Britain, although it is somewhat less developed than in the US alt-right. It was seen in action during the UK's 2017 general election, when sites such as the Skwawkbox, Another Angry Voice and The Canary rose to prominence. Then, in July 2018, the House of Commons Digital, Culture, Media and Sport Select Committee released a report on disinformation and fake news. They correctly identified that 'arguably more invasive than obviously false information is the relentless targeting of hyperpartisan views, which play to the fears and the prejudices of people, in order to alter their voting plans'.

Jim Waterson, when political editor of BuzzFeed News UK, noted that hyperpartisan websites' approach 'to news stories, where almost every action has an ulterior motive and the lines between activism and journalism are blurred, is incredibly effective at building an audience'.

In all these cases, those behind these kind of sites are unapologetically pushing an agenda and clearly see their work as balancing out the flaws they think mainstream outlets have – a recurring theme in this discussion.[25]

They also often step over the already-blurry line and stray from this highly partisan style of journalism into outright activism. In June 2018, in a profile of far-left pro-Corbyn writer and activist Ash Sarkar, the *Times*' Lucy Fisher claimed that Corbyn's office 'co-ordinates these trusted commentators through a WhatsApp group'. The group is widely believed to have existed by those in Westminster media circles. This goes beyond the usual media practice of having well-placed sources and supportive commentators, and renders the traditional line between journalism and activism almost redundant.[26]

I would argue that one of the big ways these new outlets differ from their mainstream counterparts is that they leave little of the traditional separation between opinion journalism and news reporting in place. This clear divide has historically been a key tenet of how newspapers operate and is now gleefully disregarded by upstart outlets.

In my opinion, it goes beyond what commentators and columnists, people paid to give their informed or interesting opinions, do. However, Beckett disagrees, telling me that far from this merging of news and views being new, British newspapers 'are already doing quite partisan narratives'. He

25. https://www.buzzfeed.com/jimwaterson/the-rise-of-the-alt-left?utm_term=.ouaM5AWJk#.mrYjewxB1
26. https://www.thetimes.co.uk/article/meet-ash-sarkar-britains-loudest-corbynista-lcx6hwp9t

suspects that fake news has less of an effect in the UK, 'partly because the market is already quite saturated'.

'You can look at the *Guardian* and the *Mail* doing the same story, with the same facts, and they'll have completely different narratives. One will be "this is a great thing, it's marvellous"; the other would be "this is a disaster". Now that's quite a hyperpartisan take,' said Beckett.

I think this overstates the issue somewhat. While British newspapers do clearly have editorial lines – institutionally held opinions put forward by the newspaper – they also maintain strict divides between editorials, opinion pieces and news. In print and online, those sections are separate and clearly defined. It is hard to imagine traditional journalists at mainstream outlets campaigning in the vigorous way certain new media stars do.

However, without doubt, Beckett has a point. A newspaper's editorial line clearly has a significant bearing on the way it approaches stories and even what stories it chooses to cover. Newspapers also regularly run high-profile, and often worthy, campaigns on issues and give endorsements to political parties during election campaigns. They sowed the seeds for what has since emerged online.

Similar issues apply across the Atlantic, where broadcasters in particular are not compelled to be balanced in the way their UK counterparts are. It seems plausible that the existence of this kind of partisanship in mainstream media made it more digestible to consumers when new media outlets started displaying it in a more extreme way.

Ironically, the strict rules that apply to them mean that UK broadcasters face a different kind of issue in balancing news and views. Unlike print and online media, these broadcast outlets must present issues in an unbiased and balanced fashion. Consequently, television and radio producers frequently have to deliver a debate on a topic between two or more differing voices, indicating there are two or more equally legitimate views. But this might not always be the case. Sometimes things are just wrong. Presenting balanced debates might help keep the regulator at bay, but the reliance on this format provides opportunities for liars and charlatans to gain airtime, prominence and credibility.

While Burley concedes that these so-called discos on television '[feel] to me a slightly tired way of doing things and maybe it would be refreshing to change it a bit' – something he has tried to implement in 2018 by shaking up the format of the BBC's daytime politics coverage – he is clear that it still has its place as an option for bringing an issue to viewers. He says that setting up a discussion as a head-to-head 'definitely often works, because it's a way of enlivening an issue and there is disagreement around an issue'.

I would argue, though, that all too often it encourages participants to take a more extreme position on a topic than they otherwise would. Having been involved in many of these television discussions, I can see how it would be tempting for a guest, wanting to pick up an appearance fee and get the publicity of a television interview, to talk themselves into a more hard-line stance to be more appealing to the producers. Being middle-of-the-road and conciliatory often will not get you the gig. Disagreement will. But for some topics, such a divisive approach is not always appropriate.

Burley himself says: 'What I think would be interesting is more opportunity for conversation that's around things and less argument in terms of left and right, and more discursive stuff.' Hosting more discussions in this way would certainly allow viewers to see different sides of an issue and remove some of the political polarisation that has fuelled so much post-truth thinking.

Interestingly, he notes that 'some of the research about what younger audiences are interested in, what they prefer, is they like resolution and a sense of collaboration. So funnily enough, actually – which goes against the sort of "oh, social media, everyone's at each other's throats" – is that younger audiences, some of the evidence seems to suggest, don't like that.'

It is possible that people claim they prefer this more refined way of having issues discussed on television but would actually soon become bored. However, at the moment, Burley says that he '[doesn't] know where [viewers are] being offered the alternative' to the Punch-and-Judy-style debate. He cites a video the BBC did and posted online as a rare example. The video showed a discussion between an older man and a younger man on the issue of votes at sixteen. They started off on opposite sides of the debate, and in the end they agreed lowering the voting age to seventeen might be a good compromise. Burley noted the video was well received online, so perhaps there is hope after all.

There is also the moral conundrum of defining the line between free speech and allowing people to spread lies. Is it for TV producers and presenters to define what is true or not? This was a key issue, for example, when the leader of the far-right, racist, British National Party, Nick Griffin, was invited onto the BBC's *Question Time* programme in October 2009 alongside mainstream politicians and pundits. Many asked whether Griffin should be given such a platform, while some contended it was free speech and the other members of the panel should defeat his vile views with argument.

Griffin also managed to deploy some post-truth tactics, trying to play the victim and dodging questions, claiming answering them would lead to his arrest. This was despite Labour's Jack Straw, also on the panel and serving as justice secretary at the time, guaranteeing this would not happen and demanding to hear his views. In the end it looked like the likes of Straw and the Liberal Democrats' Chris Huhne were bullying Griffin instead of holding him to account, to the extent they risked building sympathy and even support for him. The current lack of trust in mainstream journalists and politicians means that attempts to hold such people to account, to point out their lies, have become less and less effective, whatever the format.

The polarisation of politics has been an essential element in the development of the post-truth era. If people are either good or bad, right or wrong, friend or enemy, it makes it easier to dismiss what your 'opponents' say and believe whatever your side says. Politics, by its very nature, is about a variety of people putting forward their differing viewpoints. Nevertheless, there are hard facts and actual realities on the ground. By presenting information in this ideological, hyperpartisan way, that is lost. It makes people less able to consider the views of those who approach an issue differently, and ultimately it weakens political discourse.

REPEAT AFTER ME

It is easy to see how, in such an environment, consumers can limit themselves to reading and hearing the same information continuously and only encounter news and views that correspond with their own. In this era, people can easily get by without being exposed to the counterarguments to their own point of view. They find themselves, unwittingly or otherwise, trapped in something of an echo chamber that it takes proactive effort to break out of.

This is hugely significant, as information becomes more believable the more often you hear it. In 1977, the academics Lynn Hasher, David Goldstein and Thomas Toppino conducted research in which they asked college students to judge 60 statements as true or false. They picked 140 statements that seemed plausible but that most students were unlikely to know to be fact or fiction. The researchers asked students to judge the validity of these statements on three different occasions, with two-week breaks between sessions. Twenty of the statements were repeated at each session.

They found that 'repeated statements are more likely to be judged as "true" than are similar, non-repeated statements'. They concluded that their research 'demonstrated that the repetition of a plausible statement increases a person's belief in the referential validity or truth of that statement'. Hasher, Goldstein and Toppino said the results of their research showed that the frequency with which the experiment's subjects heard a statement 'must have served as a criterion of certitude'.[27] The more times you hear a statement, the more validity you give it – the more you believe it to be true. The effect has become known as 'illusory truth'.

In May 2017 psychologists Gordon Pennycook, Tyrone Cannon and David Rand wanted to see the relationship between the illusory truth effect and fake news. They found that 'the scope and impact of repetition on beliefs is greater than previously assumed' and that something being totally implausible does not act as a barrier to people believing it, if the statement is repeated sufficiently often. Indeed, they found that 'despite being implausible, partisan and provocative – fake news headlines that are repeated are in fact perceived as more accurate'. They concluded: 'Our evidence that the illusory truth effect extends to implausible and even politically

27. Lynn Hasher, David Goldstein and Thomas Toppino, 'Frequency and the Conference of Referential Validity', *Journal of Verbal Learning and Verbal Behavior*, 16 (1) (1977): 107–112.

inconsistent fake news stories expands the scope of these effects.'[28] Even a story that seems unrealistic becomes more believable to someone if they hear it repeated.

Yale psychologist Gordon Pennycook told Vox.com that 'even things that people have reason not to believe, they believe them more' if they have heard them repeatedly.[29] People believing there is no smoke without fire has left everyone burned.

Connected to all this is the idea of *truthiness*, a word and concept made famous by the American satirist Stephen Colbert. It is defined as 'the quality of seeming or being felt to be true, even if not necessarily true'.[30] The *New York Times* linguist Ben Zimmer noted in 2010 that the word had 'already appeared in the *Oxford English Dictionary* under the adjective *truthy*' before Colbert made it famous. Repetition makes things just feel more likely, then, more truthy.

Along with Trump advisor Kellyanne Conway's infamous assertion that White House press secretary Sean Spicer was simply giving 'alternative facts' about how many people attended President Trump's inauguration, this word seems to sum up the post-truth era perfectly.

Even having prior knowledge does not protect against the power of repetition. Vanderbilt University psychologist Lisa Fazio conducted an experiment that suggested 'that people sometimes fail to bring their knowledge to bear' if they understand a statement easily, even if it is false. She told Vox

28. https://www.researchgate.net/profile/Gordon_Pennycook/publication/
317069544_Prior_exposure_increases_perceived_accuracy_of_fake_news/links/
5a383377458515919e71f01f/Prior-exposure-increases-perceived-accuracy-of-fake-
news.pdf
29. https://www.vox.com/science-and-health/2017/10/5/16410912/illusory-truth-
fake-news-las-vegas-google-facebook
30. https://en.oxforddictionaries.com/definition/truthiness

that if you hear a statement two or three times, 'your brain misattributes that fluency as a signal for it being true'.[31]

We see this phenomenon playing out clearly in our current politics. A politician makes an outrageous statement – pick from the many President Trump made during his 2016 election campaign, for instance. Supporters of that particular candidate or cause then also see information and stories presented in a certain way on numerous websites, ones normally aligned with their worldview. All these stories help to reinforce each other, and the effect described by Hasher, Goldstein and Toppino takes hold. These supporters can come to believe the statement, whether it is true or not and whatever they have known before.

Additionally, some will then share the information they believe to be true across networks such as Facebook, Twitter and Reddit. This not only adds further repetition for those of a similar mindset, but also people who may not normally read such sites see the stories and are consequently dragged into the echo chamber. The cycle begins again.

The power of repetition also goes some way to explaining why the bots Bradshaw described are seen as such a significant weapon in the information war. They can make, repeat and reinforce a message almost effortlessly. They make it look like the information is coming from multiple sources – huge help for certain actors who want to push specific agendas, particularly at the scale of a national government.

Repetition of misinformation is then a key way in which fake news spreads – the power of social media and partisan news means people hear the same things over and over again, and they often do not hear opposing views. The more we hear something, the more we believe it.

31. https://www.vox.com/science-and-health/2017/10/5/16410912/illusory-truth-fake-news-las-vegas-google-facebook

Most dangerous of all is that this is now happening during an age when faith in major institutions has collapsed – making the lies even more powerful.

3

Institutional collapse

It is not only technology that is powering this age of mistrust, conspiracy and lies. The pedlars of fake news could not have had so much success without the collapse of trust in, and declining support for, key institutions that have for so long been at the centre of our society.

Much of this decline has been the result of scandals caused by the institutions themselves. These include, in no particular order, the fallout from the Hillsborough Stadium disaster, the inquiry into the handling of Stephen Lawrence's murder, the Iraq War and the Blair government's so-called dodgy dossier, Andrew Gilligan's BBC report on that dossier and the subsequent suicide of weapons expert Dr David Kelly, the MPs' expenses scandal, revelations of widespread child abuse in the Church, exposure of Jimmy Savile and other powerful child sex abusers within the BBC and the phone-hacking scandal that led to the closure of the *News of the World*.

Although they took place in a variety of institutions and circumstances over a large number of years, these scandals share a few similarities. Many involved powerful people exploiting those weaker than themselves and determinedly trying to keep this wrongdoing out of the public eye. They all damaged trusted or beloved institutions, rocking the faith of the public that had previously believed in them.

In years to come we may well be able to add the Grenfell Tower tragedy, the terrible fire at a London tower block on 14 June 2017 that cost seventy-two people their lives, to this list. At the time of writing this book, the inquiry into what happened there was still in its early stages, with the full story behind the horror yet to emerge.

However, it emerged even as the fire still raged that the residents of Grenfell Tower had long felt that their concerns about the building's safety were being ignored and that the building had been allowed to be covered in flammable cladding. The anger from them at the inquiry was palpable. It was clear from the outset that the surviving residents had no trust in those in authority to find out what had happened and deliver justice.

Survivors repeatedly decried those put forward to chair the public inquiry, considering them elite and lacking understanding of the issues. When the inquiry finally took shape, there seemed to be a determination from both the survivors and the public to apportion blame more generally, not only to those who had allowed the building to be covered in this cladding, with no sprinklers and only one escape route, nor simply to those who had previously ignored the concerns raised by residents, but also to those in command of the London Fire Brigade's response (the rank-and-file fire officers were rightly and universally considered heroes for the staggering levels of bravery they displayed).

Instead of there being some comfort when there is exposure of wrongdoing, this stream of scandal makes people far more receptive to conspiracy theories. When powerful people have insisted for years that something is wrong and it is revealed to be true, or vice versa, it makes it easier for people to disbelieve what they are told in future. If people in power have lied before, why would they not do so again?

Such scandals do not merely reduce trust in the institutions where they happened. They also affect the perception of the media outlets that have covered the issues, even if they were honestly reporting the best version of the truth that was available at the time. The BBC's Rob Burley acknowledges that his organisation is 'operating in an environment where some people are less trusting of us and they don't know how to distinguish between trustworthy and untrustworthy news sources'.

James McGrory, the former spokesman for Nick Clegg and the Remain campaign and then executive director of pro-European organisation Open Britain, told me: 'I think it's quite a dangerous thing that we've got to in our society now.'

However, he also says that he appreciates why it has happened: 'I understand years of people feeling left behind. Various scandals affecting most of our institutions, from Parliament with expenses, to the police, to the BBC with various sex abuse cases, to the churches.'

As with much surrounding the debate around fake news, the root cause is not new, but it has morphed into something bigger than has ever been seen before. McGrory says that 'there's always been a healthy mistrust of people in power in Britain', which, as a liberal, he supports. However, his experience in politics, and time on the referendum campaign in particular, made him realise that 'people don't really trust anything anyone in a position of authority says'. This is not something he necessarily welcomes.

There are numbers that bear this all out. Every year, global communications firm Edelman conducts a survey looking at trust in key institutions. The 2018 survey found that trust in the UK overall had fallen by 2 per cent from the year before. Of the countries polled, only the populations of Ireland, South Africa, Japan and Russia were less trusting than the UK's. The situation was even worse in the US. The firm recorded a fall of 14 per cent, the 'steepest ever measured'. President and CEO Richard Edelman described the situation as an 'unprecedented crisis of trust'.[1]

In similar findings, the Ipsos MORI 2018 Global Advisor report found that 49 per cent of respondents in both Great Britain and the US either strongly agree or tend to agree that their 'country is in decline'. Although an improvement from the previous report in 2016, in which the reply was 69 per cent and 57 per cent respectively, it hardly makes for positive reading. The same report found that 57 per cent in Great Britain strongly agree or tend to agree that 'traditional parties and politicians don't care about people like me'. This number hit 64 per cent in the US.

That research also revealed that this institutional decline was far from just a phenomenon confined to the UK and the US. The population with the strongest feeling that its country was in decline was Brazil's (67 per cent strongly agree/tend to agree), and 72 per cent of Mexicans strongly agree or tend to agree that traditional politicians do not care about them.[2]

Back in the UK, a study released by the Centre for Policy Studies think tank in July 2018 found that only 22 per cent of people think their district council, county council, borough council or unitary authority 'acts most in [their] best interest',

1. https://www.edelman.com/news-awards/2018-edelman-trust-barometer-reveals-record-breaking-drop-trust-in-the-us
2. https://www.ipsos.com/sites/default/files/ct/news/documents/2018-09/ga_populism_-_slides.pdf

with the local parish council polling even lower at 14 per cent. The House of Commons came in at a humbling 7 per cent. Unsurprisingly, the most popular answer, backed by 30 per cent of respondents, was 'none of the above'.

That same research found that 40 per cent of respondents would 'not trust at all' in an 'elected representative or other non-elected official in the House of Commons to do the right thing' by them if they needed to contact them for any reason.

Perhaps surprisingly, students were actually the most trusting demographic – 20 per cent said they trusted the House of Commons – but the report found that the impact of education on the level of trust was significant, with only 4 per cent of those without formal education saying they had a lot of trust in the House of Commons.[3]

This growing body of research is not only a damning indictment of those institutions but reveals a mindset that encourages people to believe fake news. London School of Economics professor Charlie Beckett told me that 'it's well documented that people are sharing even when they know it's false' and that telling people they are sharing false information 'will actually reinforce their belief'. Either people will just take in the information, assuming it to be true, or, more worryingly, Beckett says that 'they'll think, well, you're telling me it's fake, it must be true, because I don't trust anybody anymore'.

This problem can manifest itself in seemingly innocuous ways. Ian Collins recalls a time he was appearing on a BBC newspaper review programme and did not mention some health legislation that had been covered in the newspapers. Somebody actually contacted him to claim that he and his fellow reviewer had been told not to discuss this story by the BBC in order to try to hide it. Collins says he tries to

3. https://www.cps.org.uk/files/reports/original/180720173103-WhoGovernsBritain.pdf

explain to people the vast size of 'the network you'd have to set up, especially with an organisation as big as the BBC' for this bizarre conspiracy to be a reality. 'You'd have to have every editor, every producer, every reporter, every booker, who would then have to tell every guest, every contributor that you cannot mention this, this, this and this.' Yet this does not deter people from believing the very worst.

While scepticism is entirely legitimate, it must be based on fact, not conspiracy. However, such is the level of mistrust that sharing fake news has now become something of a subversive political act, the equivalent of putting two fingers up to the so-called liberal elite.

Beckett says that 'people are sharing knowing it's disruptive. They know it's exaggerated, or they know it's distorted.' However, 'if they're angry about something, they'll use that as a kind of weapon to make their point'. Falsehood is now many people's weapon of choice against the institutions they are angry at, and these institutions no longer have the credibility or authority to fight back.

Before the hand-wringing becomes too intense, it is worth noting Beckett's warning that asking people whether or not they trust the media is 'pretty dumb' for a couple of reasons: 'Firstly, because what do you mean by *trust*? And also because it varies so much. People will trust the newspaper they buy, and they will distrust all the others they disagree with.'

However, that is not to dismiss the problem outright as simply one of bad surveying. Beckett says the issue 'goes back to the bigger social trends – people being more educated. It's part of your self-worth to show you're sceptical and so on, and it also plays off into a wider questioning of authority generally.' Like McGrory, he agrees that 'it's not a bad thing that people don't trust'.

I entirely agree that as a public we should remain sceptical of those in power. We should question them and hold them to account. However, there has now been a total breakdown. The foundations on which trust is built have totally collapsed.

The media remains a key means of holding power to account (although, of course, it is a powerful institution in and of itself). I will look at the ideology of fake news later on, but suffice to say for now that no liberal could advocate anything other than a situation in which the media inform the public and are free to hold power to account. Indeed, the great liberal John Stuart Mill declared in 1859 that 'the time, it is hoped, is gone when any defence would be necessary of the "liberty of the press" as one of the securities against corrupt or tyrannical government'.[4]

A further part of the problem, says Burley, is that the public are 'told by some of those untrustworthy news sources that we [the BBC] are untrustworthy and that we're biased'. While it is entirely right that the media itself must be held to account, many of those new, partisan and outright fake media outlets are all too happy to exploit this lack of trust for their own gain.

Institutional mistrust is part of their business model, and they are deemed worthier of trust by their audience because they often mirror the audience's worldview. It is much easier to trust someone who is saying something you agree with.

That is not to say this is all the fault of an overly cynical or stupid populace. Many of the institutions we would traditionally wish to trust have left themselves open to legitimate criticism from large swathes of the public. The consequences of this have often been misunderstood by those in positions of power. Burley himself concedes that the media missed the 'underlying themes in society that actually turned out to be the reasons why [Jeremy Corbyn's Labour Party] managed to go out and garner 40-plus per cent' in the 2017

4. J. S. Mill, *On Liberty* (John W. Parker and Son, 1859).

general election when he was expected to lose heavily to Theresa May's Conservative party. Still, he acknowledges that 'can't help' the established media in trying to prove their credibility against their more forthright and partisan challengers who have now entered the fray.

It is increasingly clear that this is not a tenable situation. Scepticism has given way to a total collapse in trust, and both the public and people working in these institutions must strive to rebuild this trust and restore some balance in this relationship. But before we can try to fix this, we need to understand how we have got here.

FORTY-FIVE MINUTES

To many people's minds, one of the most significant examples of fake news is the intelligence dossiers that encouraged Britain into war in Iraq alongside the US. Central to one of these infamous documents, published in September 2002, was the claim that Iraqi forces could launch a chemical weapons attack within just forty-five minutes of the order being given and that these weapons could even hit British troops stationed abroad. When this revelation first appeared on the front of London's *Evening Standard*, the effect was as dramatic as one might expect. People had already, incorrectly, been told to stock canned food and batteries for torches, conjuring all sorts of Blitz-spirit images. This new revelation made the possibility of an attack on UK assets by reviled Iraqi leader Saddam Hussein seem not only real but imminent.[5]

Then, with that front page in wide circulation, Tony Blair told the House of Commons: 'I am aware, of course, that people will have to take elements of this on the good faith

---

5. Tom Bower, *Broken Vows* (Faber & Faber, 2016), p. 292.

of our intelligence services, but this is what they are telling me, the British prime minister, and my senior colleagues. The intelligence picture that they paint is one accumulated over the last four years. It is extensive, detailed and authoritative.'[6]

The phrasing here is crucial. Blair was explicitly asking MPs to trust him and vote for military action. Given it was a matter of national security, not all the information could be made publicly available. However, Blair was using the authority of his office and of the security services to ask not just MPs but the public at large to believe what he was telling them.

In an attempt to win over sceptics, he went on to reiterate the 'forty-five minute' claim in the House of Commons, telling MPs that the report 'concludes that Iraq has chemical and biological weapons, that Saddam has continued to produce them, that he has existing and active military plans for the use of chemical and biological weapons, which could be activated within forty-five minutes, including against his own Shia population, and that he is actively trying to acquire nuclear weapons capability'.

While members of the British public going about their normal days may not have tuned in to watch the proceedings from parliament, the message doubtlessly got through – there is a real and imminent threat. Trust us, he said. Trust me. As we know, years later, such weapons were never found.

The specific, explosive forty-five minute claim, so central to Blair's case for war, was found by the Chilcot Inquiry that followed the military action to be wrong, and the intelligence was severely criticised. The inquiry's report notes: '[Defence intelligence analyst] Dr Jones told Lord Hutton that the "problems" with the 45 minutes report of 30 August "fell into

6. https://publications.parliament.uk/pa/cm200102/cmhansrd/vo020924/debtext/20924-01.htm#20924-01_spmin0

three categories". The information was "second-hand"; it "did not differentiate between ... chemical ... or ... biological weapons"; and there was "a lack of collateral intelligence".'

At this stage, one could offer a generous interpretation that Blair and the intelligence services were acting in good faith, that they legitimately thought they had the best information available and were presenting it in the best way possible, but they happened to be wrong.

However, the Chilcot Inquiry also disclosed a letter from Blair to then-US president George W. Bush in which he said: 'I will be with you, whatever.' The letter was dated long before the final research dossier and ultimate decision to go to war and endorsed many people's view that Blair had already decided to take action and encouraged or promoted intelligence findings that supported that course.

Ultimately, the trust that Blair asked for was found to have been unwarranted.

The Iraq War also had a profound effect on how people regarded the media. Tensions had been running high between the Blair government and the BBC in the run-up to the war and remained high throughout the conflict. Head of media and strategy Alastair Campbell complained bitterly to the director of news, Richard Sambrook, on twelve occasions. Blair himself complained to the director general, Greg Dyke, and the chair of the BBC governors.

Far from de-escalating at the end of the war, those tensions erupted when, on the *Today* programme on 29 May 2003, Andrew Gilligan explosively accused the government, under the guidance of Campbell, of 'sexing up' the forty-five minutes dossier from September 2002.[7] It later emerged that Gilligan

7. https://www.channel4.com/news/articles/politics/domestic_politics/ alastair+campbell+versus+andrew+gilligan/3498447.html

had based this report on the word of a single source, the government scientist and former weapons inspector Dr Kelly, who subsequently committed suicide.

The Hutton inquiry into Dr Kelly's death used a very strict definition for *sexing up* – adding to the dossier 'items of intelligence known or believed to be false or unreliable to make the case against Saddam Hussein stronger'. It cleared Campbell of doing that, whilst blasting the BBC.[8]

In the conclusion to his report, Lord Hutton said that he considered the allegation that the report was sexed up, as the audience listening would have understood it to mean, to be 'unfounded'. He said it 'was not the case' that intelligence known to be false had been added to the dossier. He was hardly more forgiving about other elements of Gilligan's report.[9]

Writing in July 2016, Ian Burrell, then media editor of the *Independent*, correctly noted in a column: 'So much of the current public distrust in the media and its incestuous relationship with the political establishment can be traced back to its failures in covering the Iraq war.' He concluded that 'where once its access to Westminster corridors was its most valuable currency, that cosy relationship means it is now too often seen as a mere mouthpiece for the ruling elite'.[10]

In March 2018, as we approached the war's fifteenth anniversary, *Guardian* columnist Gary Younge noted the profound shift the Iraq War had caused in British politics. He outlined perfectly how it produced the lack of trust that is the perfect environment for fake news. He noted a survey that

8. Anthony Seldon, *The Blair Effect* (Little, Brown and Company, 2001), pp. 98–104.
9. https://webarchive.nationalarchives.gov.uk/20090128235523/http://www.the-hutton-inquiry.org.uk/content/report/chapter12.htm#a90
10. https://www.independent.co.uk/voices/chilcot-report-iraq-war-inquiry-media-failed-us-now-it-faces-the-consequences-a7120631.html

showed a year after the invasion of Iraq, 60 per cent of Brits said they had lost trust in ministers. Close to a decade later, the Economist Intelligence Unit argued that Britain was 'beset by a deep institutional crisis' in a report. It said the public's trust in parliament and politicians was 'at an all-time low'. Furthermore, Younge noted, the 2013 British Social Attitudes survey concluded: 'Those who govern Britain today have an uphill struggle to persuade the public that their hearts are in the right place.'[11]

It is also worth noting other ways the fallout from Iraq continues to shape our politics in the post-truth era. The Iraq War had a profound effect on the debate within the Labour Party, reflected in the way the party has increasingly moved to the left. The Stop the War coalition that formed in the run-up to the Iraq War provides a significant base of support for Corbyn, who acted as a figurehead for the organisation until he won the party leadership. It is notable that he used his response to the Chilcot Inquiry to apologise for Labour's role in the war.

So dominant does the spectre of Iraq remain in British politics that in the wake of the release of the inquiry's report, Labour shadow cabinet member Jon Trickett told a rally organised by the pro-Corbyn Momentum group: 'Our party must never again be led by someone who is unrepentant in their record supporting war.'[12]

Understanding the centrality of opposition to the Iraq War for Corbyn and his supporters is crucial to understanding how they deal with information and spread fake news. They believe that they were vindicated over the Iraq War, that their

11. https://www.theguardian.com/commentisfree/2018/mar/29/iraq-war-poisoning-national-life-corbyn-brexit-britain-vietnam
12. https://www.theguardian.com/uk-news/2016/jul/06/labour-iraq-war-leader-corbyn-trickett-momentum-rally

scepticism was proved correct then and that this can happen again.

Corbyn-supporting columnist Owen Jones summed up this view perfectly following the release of the Chilcot Inquiry's report. Writing in the *Guardian*, he said that the report should encourage people to challenge authority more boldly, be more sceptical of claims made by the government and other officials, and push back against the media. 'Lessons must be learned, the war's supporters will now declare,' he raged. 'Don't let them get away with it. The lessons were obvious to many of us before the bombs started falling.'[13]

As well as revealing the left-wing approach to Iraq, Jones provides a further indication of how the Iraq dossier damaged trust in the media, leaving many feeling that much of the media had simply regurgitated the government's line instead of scrutinising and questioning it.

He wrote that the anti-war movement was 'belittled, not least by media that largely backed the rush to war'. The media is seen as complicit, as much responsible for the horrors that happened in Iraq as the politicians and generals who made the decision to invade. To Jones and his Momentum comrades, the issue is simple – the left was right about Iraq, and the media unquestioningly spun the government's line, leading to death, destruction and disaster. None of them can ever be trusted again.

Powered by their own sense of righteousness, not least following the Iraq War, the British left sought to create a different kind of media and have largely succeeded, launching the hyperpartisan outlets we discussed earlier. One response to fake news is more fake news, and for many, the Iraq War was the launch pad.

---

13. https://www.theguardian.com/commentisfree/2016/jul/07/blair-chilcot-war-in-iraq-not-blunder-crime

HILLSBOROUGH – THE TRUTH

On 15 April 1989 Liverpool fans attended Sheffield Wednesday's Hillsborough Stadium to watch their side take on Nottingham Forest in the FA Cup semi-final – two big teams competing in a high-profile match. The pens at the stadium's Leppings Lane end, where the Liverpool fans were situated, quickly overcrowded. The crush left fans choking, gasping for air. Some were hauled out to the tiers above by their fellow fans. Over 700 people were injured. Others were not so lucky. Ninety-six fans never came home – ninety-four people died on the day, with two deaths following later.

The fans blamed the police for what happened. Indeed, during the writing of this book, the police superintendent on the day, David Duckenfield, went on trial, some thirty years on from the incident.[14] The fans believed that the police at Hillsborough that day allowed too many people into the same pens and failed to open different gates to allow fans to move elsewhere and help relieve the pressure. The police were also accused of not responding quickly enough as the disaster unfolded.

The ire towards the police started even during the incident. Liverpool's goalkeeper at the time, Bruce Grobbelaar, was defending the goal at the Leppings Lane end in the first half and consequently was the closest player as the crush occurred. He recalls going over to retrieve the ball from behind his goal and hearing fans pleading for his help, crying out: 'They're killing us, Bruce. They're killing us.'[15]

The allegation, as the *Times*' football writer Henry Winter laid out in a column following the conclusion of a second

14. The following section is based on publicly available information, and does not present risk of serious prejudice or impediment.
15. https://www.thetimes.co.uk/article/justice-cannot-heal-pain-for-families-whose-hearts-will-forever-be-broken-3gcj6mmt0

inquest, was that during the crush, 'the police then froze … inhibiting the rescue operation'.[16]

The death and devastation that day were bad enough. But instead of investigating the horror and then either addressing the criticisms or providing evidence to refute them, false stories circulated about what had happened, and were published, most infamously, in the *Sun* newspaper. The claims included that the Liverpool fans had attacked the police as they tried to help the injured, stolen from their fellow fans and urinated on authorities while they were trying to help.

These claims prompted the paper's front page four days after the horror, on 19 April 1989, to run with the infamous headline – 'The Truth'. The story, of course, was anything but. It was totally wrong.

Following that *Sun* front page, the story that the fans had caused the fatal crushing persisted for decades. That second inquest, which took place between 2014 and 2016, resulted in six senior police figures being charged in 2017. The families had campaigned on slogans such as 'nobody should be able to hide behind their uniform', believing the finger of blame should be pointed at the police.

It is almost impossible not to empathise with the Liverpool fans and share their sadness at what happened that day. As Winter wrote: 'It was the Liverpool fans who were the heroes, leaning over from the tier above, pulling people to safety. It was Liverpool fans who were on the pitch, trying to resuscitate their friends. It was Liverpool fans who grabbed advertising hoardings to use as stretchers as the ambulance service reaction was insufficient.' That is far from how they came to be portrayed.

The police's alleged behaviour following the Hillsborough tragedy has had a hugely detrimental effect on the trust the

16. Ibid.

public feel towards them. As former police chief Lord Stevens wrote with Jennifer Brown for the LSE in April 2016: 'When police do get things so badly wrong, as in the Hillsborough case, the effects are very damaging to public confidence and erode trust.'[17]

Lord Stevens and Brown wrote that the Ipsos MORI tracker of trust in professions found 'over two-thirds of those polled consistently indicate they trust the police to tell the truth', but they also noted a report by the Independent Police Commission that 'found that trust falls away the greater the engagement a member of the public actually had with the police'.

Things hardly improved following incidents like the murder of Stephen Lawrence, which resulted in the Metropolitan Police being branded as institutionally racist for its failures during the investigation.

In tandem with the falling public perception of the police, the *Sun*'s initial misreporting and its failure to apologise for those errors for so long caused huge damage to the trust in that paper and the media in general. Indeed, to this day the tabloid is largely not sold in Liverpool, such is the resentment towards it after its coverage of Hillsborough. A fulsome apology from the paper in 2012 following an independent report into what happened at the semi-final did little to dissipate the anger. Even away from Merseyside, the incident is regularly thrown back at the paper decades later, and it can easily be cited as an example of tabloid excess and lies.

What brings the *Sun*'s coverage of Hillsborough firmly into the realm of fake news, as opposed to just being bad reporting with an insensitive headline, is that it was based on a pre-existing bias, something both author James Ball[18] and Winter

---

17. http://blogs.lse.ac.uk/politicsandpolicy/police-scandals-and-cop-culture/
18. James Ball, *Post-Truth* (Biteback, 2017), p. 97.

rightly highlight. The *Sun* was much in favour of law and order, with a very pro-police stance. This editorial line made them more inclined to blame the fans.

There is also a more uncomfortable element that contributed to the way the Hillsborough coverage played out. On that fateful day in 1989 the Liverpool fans were absolutely not to blame for the crush that took place and the subsequent deaths, nor did they attack police or steal from the dead. However, their previous behaviour had earned them a reputation for hooliganism. This may or may not have had consequences in how police reacted on the day. What it did mean was that the accusations made against them after Hillsborough, unquestioningly published by the *Sun*, were easier to spread and believe than they may otherwise have been.

Specifically, just four years before Hillsborough, in 1985, Liverpool fans had been involved in a similar crushing incident. It occurred at the Heysel Stadium in Belgium, and they were to blame. Their hooliganism led to that crush, in which thirty-nine people, mostly Italian followers of Liverpool's opponents, Juventus, were killed. There is no dispute over who caused the crush that night, and fourteen Liverpool fans were convicted of involuntary manslaughter following the incident. Indeed, in 2005, when the two sides met once again, Liverpool fans approached the Juve fans with a banner emblazoned with the words *memoria e amicizia*, meaning 'in memory and friendship', as an act of commemoration, contrition and apology.[19] The Heysel incident led to English teams being banned from European football competitions for a number of years.[20]

Following Heysel, even though Liverpool fans this time

19. https://www.theguardian.com/football/2005/apr/06/
championsleague200405.championsleague
20. https://www.bbc.co.uk/news/uk-england-merseyside-32898612

were the victims, it was all too easy to believe they were in the wrong once again. Indeed, the Football Association's then chief executive Graham Kelly has admitted that, as he watched the calamity unfold at Hillsborough, his initial thought was that 'it was a behaviour problem rather than a safety problem'.[21]

Scepticism is essential to fighting fake news, falsehoods and post-truth smears, like those thrown at Liverpool fans following Hillsborough. In the immediate aftermath of the incident the *Sun*'s then-editor Kelvin MacKenzie and the man running English football at the time, to name but two, failed to show any scepticism at all. They simply appeared to believe what was circulating.

Compounding the problems years later, the *Sun* failed to put its coverage of the inquest verdict on its front pages. The paper was arguably in an impossible position. Even following its apology in 2012, no coverage of the verdict would have helped heal the wounds cause by its original reporting. However, leading with a picture of pop star Rita Ora and a none-too-convincing story about how David Cameron was handling EU negotiations policy looked callous, to say the least.

Worse came from its stablemate, *The Times*. Britain's paper of record failed to make any reference on the front page of its first edition to what was undoubtedly the biggest story that day. This was despite it being on the front page of every other paper in the country and *The Times* having the aforementioned essay from Winter, alongside other reporting, inside the paper. Following a backlash both online and, reportedly, from staff,

21. https://www.thetimes.co.uk/article/justice-cannot-heal-pain-for-families-whose-hearts-will-forever-be-broken-3gcj6mmt0

this was changed for later editions. However, the damage was well and truly done.[22]

But this goes beyond newsroom disputes and outrage on Twitter over a specific day's front page. For thirty years the families of those who died at Hillsborough led a vocal campaign in memory of their loved ones. The result of the incident was that many would never trust the police, nor the media reporting on incidents, ever again.

PHONE HACKING AND FALSE HOPE

It is hard to overstate the damage to the British newspaper industry that resulted from the *News of the World* phone-hacking scandal. An industry that was not exactly popular in the first place following incidents like the Hillsborough coverage was now definitively at the bottom of the pile. Newspapermen and women were considered little more than law-breaking, cheating abusers of privacy by large swathes of the public, a far cry from the bastions of truth that journalists saw themselves as.

The papers owned by Rupert Murdoch, his best-selling Sunday tabloid the *News of the World* in particular, were at the centre of the scandal. However, it ultimately engulfed almost the entirety of the British media and saw the likes of the *Mirror* and its former editor Piers Morgan also dragged in. Indeed, it took until December 2015 for the Crown Prosecution Service to announce that it was dropping its case against Morgan, as there was 'insufficient evidence'.[23]

I think it is fair to say that people have long been aware

22. https://www.pressgazette.co.uk/former-times-night-editor-liz-gerard-on-papers-monumental-error-over-hillsborough-inquest-coverage/

23. https://www.independent.co.uk/news/media/phone-hacking-no-further-charges-after-crown-prosecution-service-finds-insufficient-evidence-for-a6769166.html

that tabloids publish somewhat over-the-top stories or, as Ian Collins puts it, 'transfer rumours, showbiz, *National Inquirer* type stuff... "Freddie Star ate my hamster".' Essentially, these were stories that fell into the famed category of 'too good to check', and readers were mostly in on the joke. However, essential to this joke being funny was that those same readers felt they could also rely on those same newspapers for real, substantive reporting, confident that reporters had worked hard to bring them the serious information when it mattered.

The phone-hacking scandal shattered that trust between reporters and readers, with behaviour exposed that many in the public increasingly saw as beyond the pale. As the saga played out, it became clear that this was not journalists simply pushing the limits of the law for powerful pieces of investigative journalism, it was invading people's privacy to fill gossipy column inches and sell newspapers.

One of the most critical moments in the entire scandal came when the *Guardian* reported that the *News of the World* had intercepted and deleted a message on the phone of missing teenager Milly Dowler. The report, which went online on 4 July 2011 and led the next day's paper, claimed *News of the World* journalists had hacked Dowler's phone as family, friends and the police desperately tried to find her. They said that finding there was new space in Dowler's voicemail inbox, which had previously been full, gave her parents hope that their daughter was alive and checking her phone:

'The *News of the World* illegally targeted the missing schoolgirl Milly Dowler and her family in March 2002, interfering with police inquiries into her disappearance, an investigation by the *Guardian* has established.'[24]

24. https://www.theguardian.com/uk/2011/jul/04/milly-dowler-voicemail-hacked-news-of-world

The report went on to claim:

> 'With the help of its own full-time private investigator, Glenn Mulcaire, the *News of the World* started illegally intercepting mobile phone messages. Scotland Yard is now investigating evidence that the paper hacked directly into the voicemail of the missing girl's own phone.'[25]

It then detailed how *News of the World* reporters soon discovered that Dowler's voicemail inbox had become full with messages from friends and family trying to get in contact. The claim was that the journalists, desperate for new information on the case that was gripping the nation, deleted messages so new ones could be saved, causing the moment of false hope.

The fallout from the story was as quick as it was devastating. The public may have had only limited sympathy for celebrities whose privacy had been violated, but a missing schoolgirl and her despairing family were another matter altogether. Within days, the *News of the World* was no more as advertisers came under huge pressure and abandoned it in their droves.

Ironically, given that we are looking at the issues of post-truth, everything is not quite as it seems with this devastating story. Firstly, the dates involved indicate that Mulcaire himself may not have been involved in the hacking or deletion that led to the false hope moment. While the police believe the false hope moment happened on 24 March 2002, Mulcaire says he was not assigned by the *News of the World* to look into the Dowler case until 10 April.[26]

He has always insisted it was not him that deleted messages from Dowler's phone and caused the false hope moment.

25. Ibid.
26. James Hanning, with Glenn Mulcaire, *The News Machine: Hacking the Untold Story* (Gibson Square Books, 2014), p. 189.

Indeed, as a committed family man, he has said he was utterly devastated by the suggestion that he may have caused such pain to an already grief-stricken family.

Then, six months after the original story in 2011, the *Guardian* wrote in their 'Corrections and Clarifications' column:

'An article about the investigation into the abduction and death of Milly Dowler (*News of the World* hacked Milly Dowler's phone during police hunt, 5 July, page 1) stated that voicemail "messages were deleted by [NoW] journalists in the first few days after Milly's disappearance in order to free up space for more messages. As a result friends and relatives of Milly concluded wrongly that she might still be alive." Since this story was published new evidence – as reported in the *Guardian* of 10 December – has led the Metropolitan police to believe that this was unlikely to have been correct and that while the *News of the World* hacked Milly Dowler's phone the newspaper is unlikely to have been responsible for the deletion of a set of voicemails from the phone that caused her parents to have false hopes that she was alive, according to a Metropolitan police statement made to the Leveson inquiry on 12 December.'[27]

Fake news by the *Guardian*? That may be pushing the phrase to such an extreme that it becomes meaningless. New evidence emerged constantly as the investigations into phone hacking went on. To this day nobody is entirely sure what caused the deletions that gave the Dowlers false hope.

It is also right to say that the *Guardian* reporters did not deliberately falsify information in order to attack a much-hated rival – indeed, as the clarification makes clear, the *Guardian* itself reported on the new evidence found by the police. Furthermore, Lord Justice Leveson, who chaired the inquiry prompted by the

27. https://www.theguardian.com/theguardian/2011/dec/20/corrections-and-clarifications

phone-hacking scandal, said in his report 'that the essential gravamen of the *Guardian*'s original story of 4 July 2011, namely that Milly Dowler's phone was hacked by or on the instructions of journalists employed by the *NoTW*, was correct'.

However, some crucial specifics in that story were not correct. There can be little doubt that the paper would have been very keen to believe such a powerful story about one of the key assets in the empire of their bête noire, Rupert Murdoch. By the time a more accurate picture had emerged, the *News of the World* was closed, with a number of journalists losing their jobs.

To this day, many still reference the false hope story and believe it to be true. It was a key turning point, and people still blame *News of the World* journalists for allowing Milly Dowler's parents to believe their daughter may still have been alive.

Following the phone-hacking saga, the Leveson Inquiry was constituted, which very publicly hauled the media industry over the coals. Ian Collins says that 'Leveson, I think, was probably a bit of a springboard' into a collapse in trust of the media and the rise of fake news. There is certainly something in that. Edelman's annual Trust Barometer Survey recorded a 14 per cent decrease in trust towards the media in the UK in 2013, following the release of the Leveson Inquiry,[28] meaning two-thirds of the British public did not trust the media at that point.[29]

The campaign group Hacked Off was also set up in response to the phone-hacking scandal. It used legal, media and traditional campaign routes to keep up the pressure

28. https://www.edelman.com/news-awards/2013-edelman-trust-barometer-finds-crisis-leadership
29. http://www.pressgazette.co.uk/media-distrusted-30-cent-britons-wake-leveson/

on the media and urge it to reform. Some would argue it wanted to hamstring the press. It remains in existence at the time of writing this book. Over the years it has been very publicly supported by high-profile celebrities such as the actors Hugh Grant and Steve Coogan. As former *Guardian* media columnist Roy Greenslade commented, Hacked Off 'punches way above its weight'.[30] Their relentless, hugely effective campaigning has helped make sure the public remains aware of press wrongdoing and deeply distrustful of current journalists, many of whom had nothing whatsoever to do with phone hacking.

With journalists ultimately ending up in prison, including Andy Coulson, the former *News of the World* editor who went on to work for Prime Minister David Cameron, the phone-hacking scandal left trust in, and respect for, the media in tatters. It has barely recovered since.

HAD ENOUGH OF EXPERTS

Many have lost faith not only in institutions, but in the people who run them too. To be an expert in certain fields used to be considered something of an achievement. It meant that you were respected and perceived to be a worthwhile voice on the relevant subject. No longer. In the post-truth era, expertise is seen as elitist and experts themselves are increasingly considered untrustworthy.

Britain's vote to leave the European Union on 23 June 2016 should be considered then a rejection of a perceived British elite as much as a rejection of membership of the twenty-eight-country body. Michael Gove, one of the leading lights of the

30. https://www.theguardian.com/media/greenslade/2017/jan/13/hacked-off-punches-above-its-weight-but-it-will-not-and-should-not-win

Leave campaign, demonstrated this perfectly during a set-piece interview on Sky News during the campaign. When asked why a number of expert figures did not support Brexit, instead of trying to counter their arguments, he declared that 'people in this country have had enough of experts'.[31]

In response, interviewer Faisal Islam, the channel's then political editor, pointed out how similar that statement was to some of Donald Trump's politics. He also commented that far from being an anti-establishment outsider, Gove is an Oxbridge graduate and the MP for a largely well-off Surrey constituency who, as the justice secretary at the time, had the title of lord chancellor.

Watching the full clip back, one might generously conclude that Gove is saying British voters do not dislike experts per se but are fed up, as he put it, with them 'getting it consistently wrong'. However, the insidious anti-intellectualism captured by that statement cannot be ignored. It is galling enough in itself, but particularly so coming from the highly intellectual and well-read Gove.

The comparison Islam made between Gove and Trump was a fair one. Speaking at an event in Wisconsin in April 2016, Trump said: 'You know, I've always wanted to say this – I've never said this before, with all the talking we all do – all of these experts, "Oh we need an expert—" The experts are terrible.'

'Look at the mess we're in with all these experts that we have,' he continued, before suggesting that if all the presidents and politicians went on holiday all year the US would be in a better position in the Middle East.[32]

31. https://www.youtube.com/watch?v=GGgiGtJk7MA
32. https://www.politico.com/blogs/2016-gop-primary-live-updates-and-results/2016/04/donald-trump-foreign-policy-experts-221528

What is more, like Gove, Trump, with his wealth and status from celebrity and business, is hardly an outsider.

The thinking these comments reveal is pervading politics and public discourse more broadly. It is causing an intellectual race to the bottom in which those with knowledge and expertise are dismissed and derided.

In this vein, in his *Spectator* column of 7 April 2018, James Delingpole wrote that 'our culture's fetishization of expertise is a dangerous thing'. Delingpole may have been trying to be provocative, and the language is certainly that, but it is something else too. *Fetishization* implies a strangeness, as if the people who want to give some credence to true expertise are a bit weird, a somewhat bizarre way to describe listening to people who may actually know what they are talking about.

The column was focussed largely on a case brought by the cities of San Francisco and Oakland against five major oil companies (Chevron, ExxonMobil, ConocoPhillips, BP and Royal Dutch Shell), which alleged that they had conspired to hide the real extent of climate change. The judge in the case took it upon himself to educate himself in climate science and was unimpressed with what the prosecution brought before him. Delingpole argues that this shows we should all educate ourselves more and ignore the so-called experts (by pure coincidence, the judge also found in favour of the point of view Delingpole shared).

In the same piece, Delingpole said he was concerned that a group of school boys he was teaching had decided to trust economists on the economic impacts of Brexit, despite Delingpole citing examples in the past in which economists had been wrong. 'We seem to inhabit a culture where critical thinking isn't the norm (if indeed it ever was),' Delingpole laments. 'Where people find it more comforting to take complex issues such as climate change on trust than do a little digging and find out the truth for themselves.'[33]

These are just a couple of notable examples of how this anti-expertise culture has gained traction. We should certainly all seek to have as much information as possible about issues we have influence on, whether or not we are judges. That does not mean we should ignore the opinions of those who spend their lives consumed by a subject. Quite the opposite, in fact. Given the increased access to expertise that exists today – papers published online, e-books instantly available and so on – we have the opportunity to take in more of what these real, genuine experts have to offer when trying to form our own opinions.

There is a large difference between a judge reading deeply into a subject he or she is adjudicating on and, say, anti-vaccine obsessives clutching discredited pseudoscience whilst putting their children and others at risk.

There are other, more tragic, cases in which we see the opinion of experts being fought over and degraded. Consider cases in which the parents of children deemed terminally ill by medical experts have entered into prolonged legal fights to demand that care continue or that different care, normally abroad, be offered.

Given their emotive nature, such cases tend to attract a lot of public attention. This is often turned to anger at and mistrust of the medical institutions engaged in caring for the children. There are some occasions, such as the case of Ashya King, when the parents are proven right – they took their son to Spain in 2014 for proton beam therapy, and they were arrested, but he eventually received the treatment and recovered fully.

---

33. https://www.spectator.co.uk/2018/04/why-a-big-oil-row-tells-us-its-time-to-stop-fetishising-experts/

In other cases, such as those of Charlie Gard and Alfie Evans, the children were so devastatingly ill that, tragically, the world-leading children's medicine institutions were unable to do anything to improve their conditions. They also did not feel transferring them for experimental treatment was in the children's best interest.

I would never accuse these desperate, grieving parents of spreading fake news. That would be incorrect, not to mention cruel. That is not what these cases are about. However, the people who latched on to these cases, who joined 'Alfie's army' and so on, often insisted that 'parents know best', i.e. medical experts do not. It may not be fake news, but it is certainly post-truth thinking. The facts simply could not persuade them that their point of view was wrong.

Writing for CNN, O. Carter Snead says: 'What began with a hospital's deadly policy against a child with apparently permanent disabilities ended with a shocking totalitarian intervention by the state, annihilating his parents' rights in order to ensure Alfie's demise.'[34] The column is written as if the case were about state-sanctioned murder, not medical and legal experts agonising over a horrendous decision.

Of course, in these situations parents do not know better than those who have done years of training and work in world-leading children's hospitals (Alder Hey in Merseyside, in the Evans case, Great Ormond Street for the Gard case). They have wishes and parental instincts that must be respected, but not expertise. Eventually the courts did find in favour of the hospitals, but after much time, trauma and expense for all involved. The high-profile nature of the cases even led to death threats against staff at the hospitals.

34. https://edition.cnn.com/2018/04/29/opinions/alfie-evans-opinion-snead/index.html

I wish to be clear here that I do not at all decry or dismiss self-learning. Quite the opposite. Experts can and do make mistakes. Consensus can be wrong and outliers can be right. We make progress because what seems implausible suddenly becomes proven – after all, for centuries it was the consensus that the Earth was flat. The point, though, is that such research, either in a professional or personal setting, must draw on what experts know, not simply dismiss it out of hand.

Politicians are also always happy to wheel out experts who endorse their points of view, of course. Such people are always brilliant and independent when they fit with someone's agenda but normally not to be trusted when they do not. It is just another example of behaviour that has turned the public off politics and has led to the collapse of the liberal–centre ground.

4

The ideology of fake news

Most of the analysis of the spread of fake news looks solely at the relevant technological developments – particularly the rise of social media. This is understandable. Technology that allows misinformation to be spread globally in an instant, especially when combined with the huge resentment and mistrust that has built up over years towards key institutions and that makes people more inclined to believe that misinformation, has clearly played a pivotal role in what has happened. There is, however, one more important part of the story that is all too often overlooked – the ideology and politics behind fake news.

It has been regularly noted in recent years how much more polarised our politics has become. As outlined elsewhere, politicians towards the far left and far right of the political spectrum have gained prominence the world over. A large part of the power of post-truth thinking comes from this backlash that we are seeing against classical liberal values. The post-truth era is a symptom that socially and economically liberal, centrist politics, the politics that I would contend have led to huge improvements in living standards the world over, have become associated with elitism and unfairness. They have been blamed for the institutional failures outlined in the previous chapter.

This is not just about trust, though. People are yearning for something different. The centrist, liberal politics that rose to the forefront of Western post-war society have come to be seen as rather passé and dull. Established political leaders talking solemnly about budget deficits and realistic growth targets simply do not cut it in the face of an onslaught from these more radical and, frankly, more exciting opponents. As those kinds of politicians become ever more successful, others follow in their wake to try to repeat the trick.

This frustration with current politics does not have to be negative. In the UK, the formation of The Independent Group, a collection of MPs who left the Conservative and Labour parties, may be seen as a more positive manifestation of trying to do politics differently. All those initially involved were moderate MPs, although, perhaps, not particularly liberal, in the classical sense. While their policy platform was only just starting to emerge at the time this book was completed, it seems fair to say they are not trying to polarise politics. Indeed, they often cited many of the issues highlighted in this book as reasons for leaving their former political homes. For example, Luciana Berger left the Labour Party after being subjected to a long-running campaign of antisemitic abuse.[1] Indeed, upon her departure Berger declared her former party 'institutionally antisemitic'.[2]

If we want to understand the post-truth era, then, we cannot focus solely on technology and declining trust in institutions

1. https://www.theguardian.com/politics/2019/feb/18/in-their-own-words-why-seven-mps-are-quitting-labour-independent-group
2. https://www.thetimes.co.uk/article/luciana-berger-interview-corbyn-and-labours-antisemitism-crisis-crgdng6w6

but must also look closely at the crucial ideological and political issues at play. They are every bit as important.

Those of us in the liberal centre assumed – wrongly, as it transpires – that we had won the battle of ideas and that the great ideological discussion of the twenty-first century had been settled in our favour. We took it almost for granted that Francis Fukuyama was right and that we had seen 'the end of history'.[3] The post-truth era shows that this unequivocally is not the case. Instead, hard-left socialism, as practised by the likes of Jeremy Corbyn and Bernie Sanders, has risen to new prominence; so has the strongman authoritarian conservatism of Donald Trump and Brazil's Jair Bolsonaro, along with increased nationalistic sympathies, particularly in Europe.

There is little doubt that the 2008 financial crash played a large part in this shattering of the broad support for liberal politics. Much has been written and said about that phenomenon already, so I shall not repeat those arguments extensively here. Suffice to say that people felt they were bearing the brunt of the fallout from the collapse of a system while many of those at fault escaped relatively unscathed. People saw the politics that had propped up this system as being as much at fault as the economic models.

What is a matter of concern for us is how fake news has been a key part of the assault on liberalism and how the post-truth era has allowed the so-called alt-right and far left to grow to such an extent that they have to be taken seriously in the mainstream media and political discussion. Politics is no longer about debating different worldviews; it has become a culture war, with truth caught in the crossfire. (As we shall see in the

---

3. Francis Fukuyama, *The End of History and the Last Man* (Hamish Hamilton, 1992); 'The End of History?' *The National Interest*, 16 (1989): 3–18. JSTOR, www.jstor.org/stable/24027184.

next chapter, creating a culture war has been a deliberate tactic by those behind key media outlets in the post-truth era.)

Those advocating this more extreme political ecosystem have, in large part, based their politics on conspiracy theory and distortion. They see the truth as upholding the current liberal elite. Theirs is a politics where emotion matters more than fact. A post-truth politics.

The root of this politics can be found in the philosophy of the post-modernists. As Matthew d'Ancona explains in his book, *Post-Truth*: 'Post-modern philosophers preferred to understand language and culture as "social constructs", political phenomena that reflected the distribution of power across class, race, gender and sexuality, rather than the abstract ideals of classical philosophy. And if everything is a "social construct", then who is to say what is false. What is to stop the purveyor of "fake news" from claiming to be a digital desperado, fighting the wicked "hegemony" of the mainstream media.'[4] There is nothing at all to stop such people, it transpires. That is exactly what they do, and politicians are cashing in.

Left-wing commentator Owen Jones exemplifies some of this as he rails against what he sees as the 'Westminster cartel' in his tellingly titled book *The Establishment*. He paints all the main UK political parties – the Conservatives, Liberal Democrats and Labour – as essentially the same, defending the hegemony of the market-based economy and current political structures.

Writing later, the similarly left-wing Eliane Glaser identifies some of the issues related to post-truth politics in her book *Anti-Politics*, in which she laments the rejection of ideology. However, she too-readily places much of the blame on the

4. Matthew d'Ancona, *Post-Truth: The New War on Truth and How to Fight Back* (Penguin Random House UK, 2017), p. 92.

shoulders of her political opponents, seeing populism as largely a problem from the right that the left have not responded to sufficiently, arguing that 'populism is crucially different on the left and on the right'. I see almost equal culpability for the rise of populism and many similarities in the extremes on both sides of the political spectrum – the so-called horseshoe theory in action.

What makes pushing back against this harder is that those on the political extremes are true believers in their causes, in political figures such as Corbyn, Trump and others. It makes them less willing to consider dissenting views or give credence to evidence that goes against what they believe. As we shall see, they have also created a politics in which people who try to counter them, including the media, are the enemy and should be mistrusted and ignored.

Interestingly, John Stuart Mill, one of the fathers of liberalism, wrote in his seminal treatise *On Liberty*: 'The dictum that truth always triumphs over persecution is one of those pleasant falsehoods which men repeat after one another till they pass into commonplaces, but which all experience refutes.'[5] As some who have critiqued his work note, Mill was actually sceptical about the concept of the truth, feeling that if something were just accepted as being correct it could become oppressive.

Indeed, Mill actually said that if no one was genuinely arguing against a given thing, it was incumbent on people to invent counterarguments. He said there should be 'fair play to all sides of the truth', indicating he did not believe in complete truths.[6] We hear some echoes of this, the idea that the truth

---

5. J. S. Mill, *On Liberty* (John W. Parker and Son, 1859).
6. Isaiah Berlin, 'John Stuart Mill and the Ends of Life', in John Gray and G.W. Smith (eds), *J.S. Mill on Liberty in Focus* (Routledge, 1991), p. 146.

can be many-sided or even subjective, in the arguments put forward by those who spread fake news today.

Even more strident in defence of the truth, and free intellectual inquiry to find truth, is the liberal economist F. A. Hayek. Indeed, he commits an entire chapter of his flagship piece of work, *The Road to Serfdom*, to the issue. That chapter has the ominous and prescient title 'The End of Truth'. It argues that planners, Hayek's primary target in the book, employ 'various forms of propaganda' to make everyone come around to their way of thinking in order that they conform with and take part in a totalitarian system. Hayek argues that such kinds of propaganda are 'destructive to all morals because they undermine one of the foundations for all morals, the sense of and the respect for truth'.[7] Hayek regards propaganda as an enemy of freedom, of liberty. If he were writing today, Hayek would surely couch fake news in the same terms. At the very least, I regard fake news and propaganda as very close relatives, if not one and the same thing.

Fake news, propaganda, call it what you will, it is always used by those who oppose liberalism. It benefits those on the political extremes, not in the liberal centre. That intellectual pioneers of modern liberalism like Mills and Hayek identified the danger of falsehood so clearly should sound a warning for liberals in the current age.

SELF-HELP: YOUR TRUTH VS THE TRUTH

Encouraged by self-help gurus, with people striving to 'live their own truth' and variations on such mottos, the idea of a subjective truth has become increasingly prominent in popular culture.

7. F. A. Hayek, *The Road to Serfdom* (Routledge, 2001), pp. 157-159.

Search for phrases such as 'living your own truth' and 'finding your truth' online and thousands of results are returned. Website mindbodygreen offers '7 Signs You're Living Your Truth', while the Huffington Post says you can 'Step into Your Truth with These 4 Simple Steps'. On Amazon, you can buy scores of books with similar phrases in the title.

No doubt such steps can be wonderful ways of drawing out an individual's courage and unique ability, but they can also make us think that the truth is personalised.

Oprah Winfrey, speaking at the Golden Globes award ceremony in 2018, which was dominated by allegations of sexual abuse against major industry figures, said: 'What I know for sure is that speaking your truth is the most powerful tool we all have.'[8]

Your truth. Not the truth.

Perhaps what the likes of Oprah mean is that everyone should have the right to tell their own story in some form. That is no doubt important. However, this phrasing muddies the waters of objectivity, undermining the idea that we are all operating on the basis of a shared set of facts, that some things are objectively true and others are false. There are, ultimately, universal truths. A constant focus on the truth as individual and personalised risks us losing sight of that.

In a similar vein, popular lifestyle writer Dolly Alderton wrote in an article about avoiding a life crisis: 'Above all else, the best way to avoid a life crisis is to put your blinkers on.' She encourages readers to 'work out what you want'.[9] This may be perfectly worthy and beneficial advice, but if people follow

8. https://abc7.com/entertainment/oprahs-inspiring-golden-globes-message-for-the-world/2879380/
9. https://www.the-pool.com/life/life-honestly/2016/17/dolly-alderton-on-tackling-a-life-crisis

it too regularly, those blinkers can distort how they see other issues or stop them seeing them at all.

The phrasing may have been made more accessible, but the subjectivity of finding your own individual truth, of putting on your blinkers, is really no different from the subjectivity of the post-modernism that d'Ancona describes. In that philosophy, the truth as it pertains to an individual is as much a social construct as the truth in general. If we can create it for ourselves, we can create it more widely, and there is then no real anchor as to what is true and what is not.

In such circumstances, who can say whether or not Donald Trump had a bigger inaugural crowd than Barack Obama, whether or not Obama is really American or whether a PR firm in London is part of a plot to remove Jeremy Corbyn from the leadership of the Labour Party?

With such an outlook, there is also the risk that those putting forward ideas we might find far more unpleasant will deploy a similar argument. A neo-Nazi might declare it 'their truth' that Jews have horns and run the world, or that African Americans are not real Americans.

The seemingly worthy calls to find your truth, then, may be doing more harm than good.

MORE THAN A FEELING

Thoughts, philosophy and ideology are as integral to the post-truth era as the technology that spreads them. They influence how we process information and how we decide what we are going to accept as true or not.

We cannot tackle fake news without appreciating that it is highly emotive. It plays on the heartstrings. People may not believe a story exactly as it is written, but if it 'feels' true, that can be good enough.

Understanding this is critical to understanding how post-truth has developed and how fake news spreads, and to beginning to understand how we may be able to solve the problem.

But first, let's see it in practice.

PART III

Post-truth in practice

5

Post-truth politics at the polls

In our globally interconnected, highly networked age, websites publishing fake news do not exist in isolation. Distorted TV debates do not simply disappear when they go off air. News copy does not, as the old saying goes, simply become tomorrow's fish-and-chips paper.

Meanwhile, outlandish views posing as news are fed into a devoted social media echo chamber, every word embraced by people choosing only to subscribe to outlets that back up the beliefs they already have. Those people pass on the quack theories to friends, family and anyone else who will listen online. Eventually they become so widespread that the bubble bursts and the false information enters into the mainstream, where it can have the most serious of consequences.

It is becoming increasingly apparent that major political debates of our time are being influenced and distorted by fake news – there are questions about the effect fake news had on both the 2016 US election and the Brexit referendum in the UK that same year – but it also alters day-to-day political debate.

Instead of trying to counteract this, some politicians and nation states are exploiting fake news for their own political motives and trying to undermine the credibility of news outlets that seek to hold them to account, sometimes threatening journalism and journalists.

Worryingly for those of us in the political centre, this anti-liberal, anti-truth backlash is having some success at the polls.

The success of post-truth politics has been demonstrated in Britain's vote to leave the EU on a largely anti-immigrant, anti-globalisation agenda (whatever some Leave advocates may claim), sold to the electorate by a campaign organisation peddling false statistics; in the election of Donald Trump and the support for his nationalistic rhetoric and his 'America First' economic posturing; and in the ascent of far-right leaders such as Norbert Hofer in Austria, Geert Wilders in the Netherlands and Marine Le Pen in France. Those three may not ultimately have won elections in 2016 and 2017 (although Hofer later became his country's minister for transport, innovation and technology), but they attracted huge support and undoubtedly shifted the debate in their countries in an illiberal, nationalist direction.

The rise from the far left of Jeremy Corbyn in the British Labour Party, and Bernie Sanders in the US Democratic Party, equally fits into this model. While they would totally oppose what emanates from the likes of Trump, Wilders and Le Pen, they are as happy as those on the far right to wear attacks on 'neo-liberalism' and 'elites' as badges of honour. Like those on the nationalist far right, these left-wing politicians advocate policies that are inconsistent with a liberal economy and a free society, dragging their parties to the populist far left.

While neither side would like it, I deliberately group the

far left and alt-right together. Their attacks on the media, mainstream political institutions and the so-called elite have far more in common than either group would ever dare admit. To coin a phrase from former UK deputy prime minister Nick Clegg in his famous 2010 general election debate: 'The more they attack each other, the more they sound like one another.'[1]

In such a political climate, those opposing these more extreme politicians can feel compelled to respond. They might attempt to emulate some elements of their more radical opponents, shifting political debate not just away from the political centre but away from reality. As Hillary Rodham Clinton articulates in her post-election memoir *What Happened*: 'No matter how bold and progressive my policy proposals were ... Bernie would come out with something even bigger, loftier, leftier, regardless of whether it was realistic or not.'

The former first lady and secretary of state says this dynamic 'left me to play the unenviable role of spoilsport schoolmarm, pointing out that there was no way Bernie could keep his promises or deliver real results'. Sanders could promise the earth and the political climate and he never had to account for how he would make good on those promises. People had decided they wanted to hear a big, bold message, whether or not the message was actually offering something achievable.

As well as warping the policy discussion, these debates quickly turned into ad hominem attacks on Clinton from her far-left opponent. Despite private discussions about avoiding personal attacks during the campaign, 'Bernie routinely portrayed me as a corrupt corporatist who couldn't be trusted,' writes Clinton.

Who couldn't be trusted.

1. https://www.theguardian.com/politics/2010/apr/15/leaders-debate-nick-clegg-tv

It was not enough just to disagree with Clinton's politics or policies and propose radical alternatives – the nature of post-truth politics required Sanders to undermine the trustworthiness of his opponent. Once could also argue that it was part of a cynical ploy – if your own policies are unrealistic, it becomes even more important to undermine your opponent personally. If you can't win the battle of ideas, you must try to win the battle of personalities.

These smears stuck despite Sanders being unable to name a time Clinton had actually changed a policy stance or voted a different way because of a financial contribution when he was challenged to do so in a debate.[2]

Sanders' online supporters, the so-called Bernie Bros, were more than happy to pile in in support of the leader of their new cult. Clinton says that criticism from Sanders and 'attacks from his supporters caused lasting damage … paving the way for Trump's "Crooked Hillary" campaign'. Undermining trust in your opponent, based on rhetoric and not reality, is post-truth politics at its most personal and runs the risk of ushering in ever more extreme leaders.

The 2017 UK general election played out in a similar fashion. Prime Minister Theresa May, a technocrat more than an ideological politician, was pushed into an increasingly illiberal, statist corner as Labour leader Jeremy Corbyn promised that if he were prime minister, all the country's ills would be fixed. He may have proudly boasted that his manifesto was fully costed, but he made lavish promises to the electorate with seemingly little real regard to consequence or reality. Labour insisted that it wanted to end the day-to-day budget deficit, the 2017 manifesto proposed things like a £250

2. Hillary Rodham Clinton, *What Happened* (Simon & Schuster, 2017), pp. 226–229.

billion National Transformation Fund and a programme of renationalisation.[3] (The cost of renationalisation, which Labour continued to push, was hotly disputed. In February 2018 shadow chancellor John McDonnell said that bringing services into public ownership would be 'cost neutral'[4] while the anti-nationalisation Centre for Policy Studies estimated in November that year that it would cost £176 billion.[5])

As Corbyn's campaign gained momentum and his rallies, Trump-like, became higher profile, May felt compelled to at least try to match his offer to the electorate. She deployed populist rhetoric and gave speeches that attacked the 'liberal elite'. Like the Bernie Bros and the pro-Trump trolls, Corbyn's online supporters became increasingly aggressive and offensive – an issue that has only continued to escalate in the months and years following the election.

Again, trust was a cornerstone of the attack against the more established candidate, with Labour particularly keen to revive its age-old refrain that the Conservatives cannot be trusted to manage the NHS. On 20 June 2018, Corbyn tweeted: 'Why should anyone, anyone anywhere, trust the Tories on the NHS?'[6] He had said similar things when addressing the Royal College of Nursing in May 2017, telling the audience: 'This election will define the future of the NHS as no other. You can't trust the Tories with our NHS. It's too much of a risk to take.'[7] It went beyond a discussion of cuts, spending and policy into an emotional one about trust. Whatever issues there may be with Britain's health service, it is also fair to say that

3. https://labour.org.uk/wp-content/uploads/2017/10/labour-manifesto-2017.pdf
4. https://www.independent.co.uk/news/uk/politics/nationalisation-cost-tax-nothing-john-mcdonnell-jeremy-corbyn-labour-uk-politics-latest-a8204026.html
5. https://www.cps.org.uk/publications/the-cost-of-nationalisation
6. https://twitter.com/jeremycorbyn/status/1009405114984095744
7. https://labour.org.uk/press/jeremy-corbyn-speech-at-the-royal-college-of/

the Conservatives were not, by any stretch of the imagination, proposing cuts to the NHS. Indeed, their manifesto proposed 'increase[ing] NHS spending by a minimum of £8 billion in real terms over the next five years'.[8]

Some supporters even created a website called canyoutrusttheresa.com, which claimed 'Theresa May will say anything to hold on to power'.

In the blue corner, the Conservatives avoided the blatant falsehoods that were seen in the Brexit referendum but arrogantly declined to show any costings for their manifesto, making it harder to hold them to account and judge their policy platform. This is a kind of post-truth politics – a politics in which people feel they do not have to show their working. Opacity breeds unachievable policy promises, degrades credibility and causes a complete breakdown in trust – the perfect breeding ground for fake news.

At May's side during this disastrous campaign were close advisors Nick Timothy and Fiona Hill. Analysing their presence is as crucial as looking at Corbyn's in considering how the election played out. So influential were these advisors that they were forced out of their jobs soon after the election by Conservative MPs furious that their party had lost its majority in the House of Commons.

The agenda they pursued should not be dismissed as simple electioneering, either. For Timothy, who co-wrote the costings-free manifesto, this was an ideological battle against liberalism that the team had started during their time in the Home Office and were continuing in Downing Street. They wanted to take Britain into the post-liberal age. They may not have exploited blatantly fake news, but the fight against liberalism that they were happy to lead had at its core the same

8. https://www.conservatives.com/manifesto

populist attack on the 'liberal elite' deployed by more extreme politicians.

Indeed, since his exit from government, Timothy has continued to espouse the anti-liberal agenda he brought into Downing Street. Writing in the *Daily Telegraph*, Timothy opines that 'economic liberals may find capitalism's "creative winds of destruction" exhilarating, but conservatives worry about the effects on families and communities'. In the same piece, he goes on to caricature liberals by saying 'they have no responsibility', dismisses 'internationalist liberals' who 'consider the nation state an anachronism' and finishes by declaring that 'the need for a reformed, post-liberal conservatism is more urgent than ever'.[9]

With the deeply religious, socially conservative Tim Farron leading the Liberal Democrats and the frequently authoritarian and opportunistic Scottish National Party trying to maintain their total domination of politics in Scotland, there were depressingly few nods to liberalism in the 2017 general election. As if to underline the point, the result of the ballot led to the illiberal, hard-line Democratic Unionist Party from Northern Ireland supporting May's Conservatives in government, in return for £1 billion from the British exchequer. The deal was in stark contrast to Nick Clegg working with Cameron in 2010 to enact policies such as the legalisation of same-sex marriage and to lift the poorest out of the burden of income tax.

Many who supported politicians like Trump, Sanders or Corbyn, or causes such as Brexit, clearly did so in order to reject a certain set of social and economic liberal values that had come to define the centre ground of the politics that

9. http://www.telegraph.co.uk/news/2017/08/10/nick-timothy-want-win-tories-cannot-free-market-fundamentalists/

they felt had failed them. To a point, it worked; both Sanders and Corbyn did rather better in their respective elections than people imagined they would, seriously hampering their opponents. Trump, of course, made it all the way to the White House.

Given the apparent electoral benefit, then, some politicians are fully embracing this moment, looking to capitalise on it. They may be reaping the rewards personally, but they are undoubtedly taking politics in a more extreme direction.

WHO BENEFITS?

As well as the collapse in trust of key political and civic institutions, the scandals outlined in the previous chapter have contributed to a near-total mistrust in the people running those institutions, both specific individuals and the type that have traditionally held those roles in general.

These individuals are increasingly seen as distant, elitist and self-serving. This may be true of some, and all institutions need fresh blood and new ideas in order to move forward, but this view rather unfairly tars everyone in public life with the same brush.

Worst of all, instead of trying to fix this problem and regain the public's trust, some in politics have actually embraced this rejection. Instead of striving to improve our politics, some politicians are cynically exploiting the public frustration to further their careers and to push their normally rather extreme worldviews.

As well as Corbyn, the UK also has the likes of Boris Johnson, Nigel Farage and Jacob Rees-Mogg. At first, these individuals may all seem quite different – certainly the political worldview of the latter three shares little with Corbyn's. What they do share is that they are all very much part of 'the establishment' but have succeeded in playing on the perception that they are genuine and authentic. This is even true when their apparent authenticity leads them to be little more than bigoted, offensive, incompetent or all of the above. They have played the outsider to capitalise on public anger and resentment and gained profile and power.

I consider Jeremy Corbyn the ultimate response to the New Labour era of Blair, Brown, Mandelson et al. His rise to the leadership was born of a desire to find the antithesis of those leaders. Amongst other things, New Labour were blamed for the disastrous war in Iraq and, at least in part, the 2008 financial crisis. Corbyn had been a vocal critic of that war specifically and a consistent rebel against the New Labour government more broadly. (Ed Miliband tried to pitch himself as a break from that past too, but ultimately he was dismissed as a close associate of Brown and as lacking the ideological purity Corbyn would later show.)

When, in 2015, Corbyn threw his name into the race for the Labour leadership, he had no belief he could actually win the contest against the likes of former home secretary Yvette Cooper or former health secretary Andy Burnham. Many speculated he did not even really want to. Still, this was no Macron-style outsider coming to shake up the political establishment – Corbyn had been an MP in the Palace of Westminster for thirty years. It was simply his 'turn' to be the far-left outrider, as allies Diane Abbott and John McDonnell had been in previous contests.

Initially, Corbyn struggled to even get enough nominations to be on the ballot. When he eventually did, he managed to sweep to victory thanks in no small part to a highly energetic grassroots campaign that overpowered the scrutiny his previous policy positions came under. It was a campaign inspired by the counterintuitive idea that the longest-serving

MP in the race, indeed one of the longest serving in the entire House of Commons, was the outsider needed to shake things up.

During the UK's tumultuous 2017 general election campaign, Corbyn came under even more intense pressure from the media (not surprising, given he claimed to want to lead the country). Story after story detailed his connections with IRA members, a failure to combat antisemitism within his party and previous speeches he'd made to Islamic extremists. This was before mentioning his reported references to terror groups Hamas and Hezbollah as his 'friends' and paid-for appearances on Iranian state television.

All this should have precluded Corbyn from leading the management committee of his beloved allotment, let alone a major political party. Far from it. In this topsy-turvy age, it just made Corbyn plain-speaking, and the papers who reported these incidents were accused of smearing him. It was deemed an affront that this apparently mild-mannered, bearded man should be held to account and proof positive that the 'establishment' was scared and trying to keep him out of No. 10.

Indeed, the media onslaught actually came to be seen as something of an endorsement of Corbyn. In the post-truth era, a substantial number of people have decided that if the press are attacking someone then it must be the press who are in the wrong, not their target. In the end, Corbyn's party surged to an unexpected 40 per cent of the vote in the election, gaining seats and depriving Conservative prime minister Theresa May of the parliamentary majority she had expected when she called the election.

Corbyn maintained his outsider schtick even as he sat as leader of the Labour Party. As Ian Collins points out, he's 'not … Bob from Arbroath who's suddenly discovered a voice,' but 'the leader of Her Majesty's Opposition. You're part of the Privy Council. And you, you know, you probably are the very group of people you're talking about.'

'He is establishment himself, albeit a different part of the spectrum, maybe,' adds Collins.

Boris Johnson, too, has benefited from being perceived as plain-speaking. His missteps and misspeaks can just be attributed to 'Boris being Boris' and seem genuine. However, everything from his somewhat bedraggled mop of blond hair to his verbose language is deliberate and highly affected.

And he too has done things that should really have discounted him as a serious political force. After eventually resigning as May's foreign secretary over her Brexit proposals, Johnson wrote a column for the *Telegraph* in which he described Muslim women in traditional head coverings as looking like letter boxes and bank robbers.[10]

Provocative, offensive and unbecoming of someone who, days earlier, had held one of the great offices of state. Again, in the political climate, it was batted away. People came out to defend Johnson as being plain-speaking and saying what people actually think. The *Sun* even published a series of letters from readers agreeing with him.[11]

He tried to charm reporters camped out on his doorstep for comment with cups of tea served in a random collection of mugs – all part of the act.

Johnson's Conservative Party colleague Jacob Rees-Mogg is in some ways an even more extreme example. The Mogg, as he is known, is seldom seen wearing anything but a double-

10. https://www.telegraph.co.uk/news/2018/08/05/denmark-has-got-wrong-yes-burka-oppressive-ridiculous-still/
11. https://www.thesun.co.uk/news/7008770/the-sun-reader-letters-boris-burka/

breasted three-piece suit, and he has admitted that on his first canvassing trips he was accompanied by his nanny.

No matter that his political views are extreme and his lifestyle unimaginable to most. His unashamed pomp and poshness has, once again, allowed him to be seen as authentic, the perfect Conservative response to Corbyn. As d'Ancona puts it in a scathing *Evening Standard* column: 'Having turned up at the fancy-dress party of modern politics as a punctiliously polite toff, he revels in the confident eccentricity that makes the English go weak at the knees.'[12]

Using Britain's negotiations to exit the EU as a way to build his profile, he succeeded in gaining a devoted following within the Conservative Party, many of whom come from a new generation of activists who see Rees-Mogg as the saviour of conservative values and free-market economics. D'Ancona adds that Rees-Mogg engaged in a 'pantomime of disingenuously polite ideological menace', pretending to be the perfect, polite English gentleman whilst attempting to bully the government into ever more extreme positions and, like Johnson, 'present[ing] himself as a good sport,' doing things like appearing on the TV quiz show *Have I Got News for You*. His authenticity appears to be little more than an act, playing a part in order to gain power and pursue his political agenda.

Whilst writing a profile of Rees-Mogg (full disclosure – the profile was written for a publication being edited by d'Ancona), I spoke to a young Conservative staff member called Sam Frost, who told me: 'Whether you disagree with [Rees-Mogg] or agree with him on issues, you probably have to agree with the fact that he is a very honest man.'

---

12. https://www.standard.co.uk/comment/comment/reesmogg-s-eccentric-side-hides-a-far-more-sinister-political-animal-a3879171.html

In the same vein, another activist, Josh King, said: 'Whether you like him or not, he's a very clear, principled person.'[13]

The supposed authenticity trumps all else.

In a discussion with Nick Clegg on his podcast *Anger Management*,[14] former chancellor of the exchequer George Osborne describes encountering Rees-Mogg for the first time when he was a student and regarding him as something of an 'alien species'. With typical astuteness, Osborne notes that, far from being authentic, all the quirks that the likes of Johnson, Farage and Rees-Mogg have that make people see them as genuine are actually highly affected and completely deliberate. They are post-truth characters for a post-truth world.

Former UKIP leader Nigel Farage operates along similar lines. Like Corbyn, he claims to be a political outsider and says that 'the establishment' are scared of him and trying to keep him from power, but he has actually sat in a parliament (in this case, the European one) for a significant number of years. He also has quirks like Rees-Mogg's and is rarely seen without a pint of beer and something to smoke. Like Rees-Mogg and Johnson, he pretends to be a good sport who can laugh at himself, but it is all a carefully constructed act.

Across the Atlantic, it is easy to see how Donald Trump fits into all this. He is the reaction to President Barack Obama in the same way that Corbyn is to New Labour. Trump bulldozed through a field of establishment Republicans during the party's primary process – Governors Jeb Bush and John Kasich, along with Senators Ted Cruz, Marco Rubio and others, were all crushed by the seemingly unstoppable Trump train. Like Corbyn, nobody is even sure that Trump wanted to win, but

13. https://drugstoreculture.com/the-acolytes-of-jacob-rees-mogg/
14. https://audioboom.com/posts/6838134-know-your-frenemy-nick-clegg-talks-to-george-osborne

he enjoyed blasting the establishment figures as he beat them, blaming them for years of perceived failings and firing up his base in Middle America.

While Trump may have been a political outsider, this is a man who knew the great and the good of New York life and lived in a gold Manhattan tower block named after himself. He is as separate from the people he claimed to represent as it is possible to be. However, like Corbyn, Trump was supported by a hardcore base of grassroots activists in his political ascent, largely online. A lot of this was based on nonsense and fake news, and some of his army of online supporters still brag that they used internet memes to propel their man to victory.

As with Corbyn, each new revelation in the mainstream media against Trump was seen as part of an establishment attack, not as legitimately holding a deeply flawed candidate to account. They made him more popular. No man who brags about sexually assaulting women should make it to the White House, and yet it did not hold Trump back; people defended him as just engaging in the type of 'locker-room talk' that 'normal' men engage in day to day. That infamous *Access Hollywood* tape which revealed those comments about 'grabbing [women] by the pussy' is far from the only thing that would have finished a normal political candidate in a normal political era, yet seemed to slide off Teflon Trump or even help him.

At Trump's side for much of this was Steve Bannon, executive director of Breitbart. He became chief executive of Trump's campaign and later joined Trump's staff at the White House. He helped hone the message that took Trump to his unexpected victory, and he brags about the nationalist policies he helped implement whilst in the corridors of power. This is a man who sees politics as a blood sport and told a *Sunday Times*

Magazine interviewer that in politics 'you gotta be a carnivore. You have to want to kill.'[15]

Unlike the Farages and Trumps of this world, Bannon came from a working-class background and served in the military. Despite the fact he also worked for Goldman Sachs and earns royalties from the US sitcom *Seinfeld*, he does appear to have some genuine empathy for the working-class people he claims to fight for – except he has used their anger to justify the racist, misogynistic revolution he wants to bring around the world. He taunts his detractors, saying he does not care about being called racist and flipping the attack on its head: in that same *Sunday Times Magazine* interview, he said that 'To make the lives of the Hispanic and black working class in this country better, one of the things you have to do is stop illegal immigration.'

This phenomenon is playing out around the world, not just on both sides of the Atlantic and in Western Europe. In October 2018, Jair Bolsonaro, previously a far-right senator of no real significance, was elected president of Brazil, the world's fourth-largest democracy. The so-called Tropical Trump's victory was inspired by the huge resentment of the current political class in that country and his offer of something different.

Bolsonaro's win was also thanks in no small part to a campaign of fake news about his opponent that was spread via Facebook and, most potently, the mobile messaging service Facebook owns – WhatsApp. WhatsApp groups that bring together a range of users are hugely popular in Brazil. Benjamin Junge, an anthropology professor at the State

15. https://www.thetimes.co.uk/article/the-magazine-interview-the-former-white-house-chief-strategist-steve-bannon-on-nigel-farage-populism-in-europe-and-trumps-visit-to-london-h6vbzc5g3

University of New York at New Paltz and a Fulbright fellow at the Federal University of Pernambuco in Brazil, told Vox that it is not just families who use WhatsApp groups to communicate: 'Every kind of like religious community, every evangelical church, every individual kind of Catholic church has a WhatsApp group. Uber drivers in different neighbourhoods and cities have WhatsApp groups, taxi drivers, students, groups of friends, teachers use WhatsApp.'

He explained that Facebook is important but 'WhatsApp is where the real frictions and kind of circulation of content is happening. And possibly where opinion formation, the actual congealing of voter sensibility, is concentrated.'[16]

Brazilian voters were clearly frustrated with their current politics, which had been dogged by large-scale corruption. It made them more receptive to the fake news backing a hard-line candidate saying he would fix all the problems. The political ideas that had previously won in post-dictatorship Brazil were associated with corruption and failure. The more conventional approach of his opponent, Fernando Haddad, simply did not cut it in the fraught political times. In the end Bolsonaro won the run-off election comfortably.

These individuals, along with a number of other culprits, are the embodiment of post-truth politics. They do not want to improve the way political bodies operate, as they should. Instead, they want to exploit the anger felt towards those institutions and turn it to their advantage so that they can win power. In the tumultuous times in which these figures are operating, people appear to be drawn to their seeming ideological certainty. They all claim to want, in the words of

16. https://www.vox.com/world/2018/10/29/18025066/bolsonaro-brazil-elections-voters-q-a

Trump, to 'drain the swamp', but they are as much creatures of the swamp as any of their opponents, if not more so.

They use well-constructed personas to appear genuine, but they are as false and contrived as any piece of fake news. D'Ancona writes that there has come to be a 'dangerous confusion of staged eccentricity with true character, and the lazy invocation of that much-abused word "authenticity". We now say that people are "authentic" when all we really mean is that they are unusual.'[17] Sure, politics may be show business for ugly people, as the famous saying goes, and politicians have to build public personas, but these people take it to the extreme and capitalise on mistrust.

The saddest thing is that we have become so desperate for some authenticity in public life after multiple scandals, Bill Clinton's deceit and the New Labour years' obsessive message control that we have fallen for these post-truth politicians' acts.

THE MAINSTREAM MEDIA

Attacks on the media are central to this political moment. When journalists have tried to question Trump, Corbyn, the Brexiteers or to hold them to account, they have all been very ready to turn on the media and try to discredit it. The media has become as much a focus for those people and their supporters as their political opponents. Attacking what they mockingly refer to as the mainstream media is all part of their supposedly radical and revolutionary politics – an attempt to overturn the existing elites.

They have turned large parts of the media into the enemy, telling people it cannot be trusted and persistently chipping away at the credibility of serious news organisations, making

17. https://www.standard.co.uk/comment/comment/reesmogg-s-eccentric-side-hides-a-far-more-sinister-political-animal-a3879171.html

it easier to dismiss any negative stories about these figures that may emerge. During his speech to the 2018 Labour Party conference, for instance, Corbyn told the party faithful: 'Here, a free press has far too often meant the freedom to spread lies and half-truths, and to smear the powerless, not take on the powerful. You challenge their propaganda of privilege by using the mass media of the twenty-first century: social media.'[18] That followed a video he had posted to a YouTube channel in response to stories about his alleged involvement with a Czechoslovakian spy back in the 1980s, a story he tried to dismiss. Seemingly liberated by his supporters' social media presence and dislike of the media, he hit back, using a YouTube video to warn the 'media barons' that they were 'right to be' worried about a Labour government. With a sinister smile, he ended the video by warning them: 'Change is coming.'[19]

It is a prime example of how this mass media of the twenty-first century can easily become a bully pulpit, used with the intention of silencing dissent.

With the boom in independent online publications – websites, YouTube channels, podcasts and so on – that Corbyn was referring to, it has increasingly become seen as elitist to advocate that the work of long-established publications or journalists should be given greater weight than the random article from a random website that popped up in your Facebook feed. Former NUJ President Tim Dawson says that his 'sense is that [for] lots of young people … the mainstream media is almost not in their vision. It's not that they don't trust it or don't like it, it's something their parents maybe looked at.'

18. https://www.pressgazette.co.uk/jeremy-corbyn-tells-labour-conference-free-press-in-uk-has-too-often-meant-the-freedom-to-spread-lies-and-half-truths/
19. https://www.youtube.com/watch?v=xIlA8Ib1NgY

Or, as Ian Collins puts it, 'when [callers to his radio programmes] say that expert is wrong on this or that that person is wrong', what they mean 'is that their mate Joe wrote a blog somewhere and they agree with him. As distinct from any qualified standpoint. That's often then interpreted not just that they disagree with an expert but actually they think there's almost a conspiracy around it.'

Those politicians, and many others, have been more than happy to exacerbate this situation offline too and encourage their followers into outright hostility towards the media, holding rallies where the journalists assigned to cover the events are booed and mocked from the stage.

Trump is the perfect example of such behaviour. He has regularly referred to journalists, with the exception of Fox News and a small group of others, as 'the fake news media'. In July 2017, six months into his tenure as president of the United States, Trump tweeted a clip of himself appearing at a WWE wrestling event in 2007 and body slamming WWE chief Vince McMahon (whose wife Linda is in Trump's administration). This would be an odd thing in itself for the most powerful person on Earth to do, but the clip had been edited by Trump supporters to have a CNN logo superimposed on McMahon's face. Trump, having seen it online, decided to share it with the millions of people who follow him on the social network.

The total degradation of the office of president aside, the incident perfectly illustrated Trump's approach to the media. He wants to attack it, pummel it, and is proud of doing so. He is happy to encourage violence against journalists. The media is his opponent and therefore it is to be beaten by him in front of baying crowds.

This philosophy has its roots in the work of people like Andrew Breitbart, the late founder of the stable of news and opinion websites that still bear his name and that did so much to create the Trump supporters of the alt-right. In his memoir, Breitbart wrote: 'I'm at war with the mainstream media because they portray themselves as objective observers of reality when they're no such thing.'[20] This war that Breitbart highlighted is central to alt-right ideology and came right to the heart of the White House in the form of former Breitbart boss Steve Bannon.

Few others have taken their dislike for the media to these levels, but it is all a matter of scale. In the run-up to the 2017 UK general election, Corbyn supporters would regularly heckle reporters who asked questions of their leader, deeming them to be biased, in a manner similar to Trump supporters. This included at least one bizarre occasion on which Labour supporters booed the political editor of the *Daily Mirror*, Britain's Labour-supporting tabloid, for asking a fairly standard, albeit probing, question.

A more high-profile incident occurred after Corbyn was skewered by presenter Emma Barnett on Radio 4's high-profile *Woman's Hour* programme. Barnett, not unreasonably, wanted to know the numbers behind the new universal free childcare programme Corbyn had come onto her programme to launch. However, the man who wanted to be prime minister struggled to answer this question. During the course of the interview he received a phone call, tried to log in to his iPad and flicked through his manifesto, all while Barnett was asking for one relatively straightforward figure. It was excruciating listening.

Of course, in the mind of the Corbyn followers, it was Barnett who was at fault. She received a tirade of abuse online, including from well-known figures such as former *Newsnight* economics editor turned Corbynista columnist Paul Mason.

20. Andrew Breitbart, *Righteous Indignation* (Grand Central Publishing, 2011), p. 58.

Indeed, the abuse of particular journalists got so bad from the so-called Corbynistas during the 2017 campaign that the BBC's political editor, Laura Kuenssberg, was assigned a bodyguard to protect her during the party's annual conference in 2017.[21] Speaking about the incident at an event run by the charity Jewish Care, Kuenssberg, the first woman to hold this prominent role, was quite clear: 'What they are trying to do is silence me.'[22] She was right. Her vicious critics wanted to intimidate, silence and discredit her. They wanted to invalidate what one of the country's most senior and accomplished journalists was reporting, as they feared it was bad for their party.

As with Trump, the landscape was created long before the frontman came to power. The prominent British left-wing writer Owen Jones, who became a very vocal supporter of Corbyn and his political platform, is one of those who helped achieve this. In his bestselling book *The Establishment: And How They Get Away With It*, Jones set out the narrative of the media as an elite to be toppled. He wrote: 'There is not a free press in Britain: there is a press free of direct government interference, which is a different thing altogether.'[23]

It is worth reiterating that a press free of direct government interference is a seminal tenet of a liberal society and not something to be easily dismissed or taken for granted in the way that he seems happy to. Jones went on to argue that 'the terms of political debate are ruthlessly policed, particularly by the tabloid media; those who fall foul of them can face crucifixion by newspaper. The media, in other words, is a pillar

21. https://www.theguardian.com/media/2017/sep/24/bbc-political-editor-given-bodyguard-for-labour-conference
22. https://www.thejc.com/news/uk-news/they-are-trying-to-silence-me-bbc-s-laura-kuenssberg-on-the-trolls-who-attack-her-1.447104
23. Owen Jones, *The Establishment* (Penguin Random House, 2015), pp. 89–90.

of the Establishment – however much many journalists may find this an unpalatable truth.'

This type of deliberate undermining of journalists doing their job by high-profile politicians and commentators is an assault on a free press and is in direct contradiction to the core values of liberalism. Those who indulge themselves by behaving like this do nothing more than undermine one of the crucial ways in which the general public are able to hold our leaders to account.

Take, for example, the case of Stephen Daisley in Scotland. Daisley was digital politics and comment editor at Scottish terrestrial broadcaster STV. He was seemingly forced out of the role after pressure was applied to his managers by senior politicians in the Scottish Nationalist Party (SNP). Reflecting on his departure in the *Scottish Daily Mail*, Daisley wrote that as he 'grew more sceptical of independence and began to question if it was just souped-up nationalism I found myself a target for the SNP's cybernats'[24] – online trolls supporting the SNP and the Scottish independence movement.

More worryingly, nationalist politicians then pushed to have him removed. They criticised him repeatedly on social media and took their complaints to the chief executive of STV at a briefing meeting he held. At the time, one of these MPs, John Nicolson, was sitting on the House of Commons' powerful Media Select Committee. Daisley was eventually told by his managers he could either continue to edit the politics page of the website or write comment but not do both (despite his title). He subsequently decided to leave the organisation. As he saw it: 'Two SNP MPs had used the bully pulpit of Twitter to lean on STV and STV had caved. And now their online politics

24. https://stephendaisley.com/2017/02/04/snp-tried-to-silence-me-and-their-freedom-to-bully-vilify-and-malign-is-a-chilling-glimpse-of-one-party-scotland/

and comment editor would no longer be allowed to edit and comment on politics online. This wasn't Kafka, it was Lewis Carroll.'

The attack on Daisley was arguably a continuation of SNP hostility to the parts of the press that challenged or disagreed with them. In September 2014, during the height of the independence referendum campaign in Scotland, supporters of independence held a protest outside the BBC's headquarters in Scotland, accusing it of bias and attacking the BBC's then political editor, Nick Robinson. The protests were backed by Alex Salmond, who was first minister of Scotland and leader of the SNP at the time.[25]

It should go without saying that journalists must be held to account as everyone else in the public eye is. However, insulting the entirety of the media, save for the bits that share your particular worldview, and damning it as untrustworthy is illiberal and antidemocratic. Politicians forcing out critical journalists is equally authoritarian and troubling.[26]

For decades, some people have argued that privately owned corporate media organisations put forward the views of a privileged minority. You can see this theory writ large in the approach of Jones and Corbyn. It has often overshadowed the more liberal idea that having a wide selection of privately owned media companies who have to compete against one another results in strong, independently funded journalism.[27]

It also ignores that under liberal free markets, people have choice, and that competition breeds quality and a range of services. It is one of the most basic rules of science that each

---

25. https://www.theguardian.com/politics/2014/sep/15/alex-salmond-bbc-protest-nick-robinson
26. Ibid.
27. Tim Luckhurst, 'Give Me the Press Barons Any Day', *British Journalism Review*, 28 (2) (2017): 33–34.

force creates an equal and opposite force, and so too does it work in free markets. The creation of Fox News produces an MSNBC, the presence of Sean Hannity means you get a Rachel Maddow, and so on.[28] The market demands that this is the case.

However, for this to work, the individual journalists and media organisations as a whole must maintain the highest standards. That this has not happened, that journalism has been undermined by issues like the phone-hacking scandal or, as Professor Charlie Beckett puts it, the way journalists have 'been thoroughly unaccountable', has led to the behaviour we are seeing from prominent politicians and their supporters. But this is a reason, not an excuse. The post–liberal leaders who try to curtail the free press for their own political ends help create a situation in which fringe outlets and conspiracy theories are given as much credence as hard news stories by credible organisations. Ultimately, it degrades our public discourse. We all lose out.

28. http://www.cityam.com/profile/charlotte-henry/archive

6

Brexit means...

£350 MILLION A WEEK FOR THE NHS

Prominent politicians representing the official Vote Leave organisation, including cabinet ministers Michael Gove, Theresa Villiers and Priti Patel, as well as the aforementioned Boris Johnson – who went on to become foreign secretary after the referendum – spent weeks campaigning alongside a bus emblazoned with the slogan: 'We send the EU £350 million a week. Let's fund our NHS instead.'

The claim was that as a result of exiting the EU, the UK would have £350 million more per week to spend on the NHS. The number was printed on leaflets, and those senior figures appeared in numerous TV packages and interviews alongside the slogan.

The campaign, however, was total fake news and came to exemplify the Leave campaign's loose relationship with the truth. James McGrory was on the front line of the Brexit battle, leading the press operation for Britain Stronger in Europe, the official Remain campaign. Even nearly three years later, it is clear that the pledge of £350 million a week for the NHS rankles him more than almost anything else that happened over that period of time.

He highlights two issues with it. The first is that 'the total amount of money that is spent before the rebate, right, so literally our net contribution, would roughly work out at £350 million a week'. However, 'less the rebate it's nothing like that'. Or, as he less charitably puts it: 'The figure ... is bullshit.'

McGrory says that 'the thing about the bus that made it in a way to me more egregious is there is an intellectual justification for what they did and put on the side of the bus, which [senior members of the Leave campaign] still to this day make, with a smile on [their] face'.

It is yet another example of a grain of truth being twisted and distorted beyond all recognition.

But, McGrory points out, the issue does not end with a dodgy figure: 'the figure itself is bullshit but the other idea that it goes to the NHS and they would have any say in doing that is also bullshit.' This is true. The Leave campaign was not a political party aiming to form a government. It was a single-issue group set up to fight one referendum and supported by people across a number of political parties.

While it is right and proper that they would want to set out a vision for the future and try to explain what would happen if they won, the idea that victory would automatically mean any of the Leave campaign would be in a position to implement any such policy is nonsense. They were not putting forward an election manifesto. The campaign, even with its high-profile backers, had absolutely no authority to say what a government would do following the Brexit vote in this manner.

So controversial did the £350 million figure become that the National Statistics Authority (NSA) actually went as far as to publicly complain about its use. The chair of the NSA, Sir Andrew

Dilnot, said he was 'disappointed' with the continued use of the figure, saying, as McGrory does, that it was Britain's gross contribution to the EU and failed to take into account what the country receives back in the form of a rebate. Sir Andrew said:

'The UK's contribution to the EU is paid after the application of the rebate. We have also pointed out that there are payments received by the UK public and private sectors that are relevant here. The continued use of a gross figure in contexts that imply it is a net figure is misleading and undermines trust in official statistics.'[1]

This is strong language indeed from a body that is traditionally very reserved, and it was not the only one. Paul Johnson, head of the highly respected economics think tank the Institute for Fiscal Studies, said: 'It is equivalent to suggesting that were the UK to leave the EU and not make any financial contribution to the EU's budget then remaining EU members would continue to pay the rebate to the UK. That is clearly absurd.'[2]

The claim even caused Conservative MP Dr Sarah Wollaston to defect and begin supporting the Remain campaign. She would later go on to be one of the first three Conservative MPs to join the newly formed Independent Group in parliament. The former GP said: 'For someone like me who has long campaigned for open and honest data in public life, I could not have set foot on a battle bus that has at the heart of its campaign a figure that I know to be untrue.'[3]

However, it did not deter those who stayed part of the Leave

1. https://www.statisticsauthority.gov.uk/news/uk-statistics-authority-statement-on-the-use-of-official-statistics-on-contributions-to-the-european-union/
2. https://www.ft.com/content/b2858ec6-21aa-11e6-9d4d-c11776a5124d#axzz4BAegkt7l
3. https://www.theguardian.com/politics/2016/jun/09/dr-sarah-wollaston-defects-vote-leave-remain-campaign?CMP=fb_gu

campaign. They continued to defend the figure and used it throughout the campaign period. Indeed, they carried on using it as a campaign slogan long after the votes were counted. More than a year after the referendum, in September 2017, some time since the number had been thoroughly debunked, Boris Johnson wrote for the *Telegraph*: 'Once we have settled our accounts, we will take back control of roughly £350 million per week. It would be a fine thing, as many of us have pointed out, if a lot of that money went on the NHS, provided we use that cash injection to modernise and make the most of new technology.'[4]

This is the thing about fake news. You cannot just push back on it once. You end up playing a kind of whack-a-mole in which untruths keep popping their heads above the surface.

This is important because as well as being misleading, fake news can also be deliberately provocative, to play on emotions, and McGrory sees the Leave campaign's use of the £350 million figure in that way. He says they knew that 'anyone who values statistics or accuracy in political debate would get quite exercised about it'.

He also says that the Leave campaign, as is so often the case with people spreading fake news, knew the detail would not be important. Instead, 'they did it deliberately, knowing that would then be a topic of conversation, knowing that then people who don't follow it like you or I follow it, sort of political geeks, all they'd really hear is "we send a lot of money to Brussels, I want to spend it on the NHS"'.

It was the emotion of the pledge, what it signified, not the reality, that mattered. Ian Collins also touches on this idea that people were attracted to the principle, not the specifics, of

4. http://www.telegraph.co.uk/news/2017/09/15/boris-johnson-vision-bold-thriving-britain-enabled-brexit/

the £350 million figure. He has publicly stated that he voted Remain, but he told me: 'I can't be the only person that never took that literally… It wasn't being said by anybody with any authority to say it.'

That is true. It is worth reiterating that the idea was put forward by a single-issue political campaign, not as part of a manifesto for government. It is therefore perfectly conceivable that some Leave voters accepted that the precise level of investment into the NHS was unlikely but still voted for Brexit because of the principles of increased funding and financial independence that the claim implied.

McGrory says at first he and his colleagues tried to ignore the £350 million claim in order to reduce the amount of attention it got. This didn't work. The figure was on the side of the official campaign bus and consequently broadcast on the news every night. 'In the end, we just felt we had to have a row,' he says. He explains that the Remain team hoped that 'some people will surely listen to the fact that this is bollocks'. However, he acknowledges that the Leave side realised that there were enough people, some of whom were vaguely sympathetic to the Remain cause, who found any sum of money going to Brussels instead of the NHS unjustifiable.

It is hard to see this as anything other than post-truth campaigning, and the man behind the Leave campaign, Matthew Elliott, has done it before. In the run-up to the UK referendum on whether to change the parliamentary voting system from first past the post to the alternative vote, he ran a campaign that again focussed on cost and spending alternatives.

It included a set of highly emotive posters, one of which featured a crying newborn baby and the caption: 'She needs a maternity ward NOT an alternative voting system. Say No to spending £250m on AV. Our country can't afford it.' Another poster displayed a wistful, handsome soldier and the caption: 'He needs bulletproof vests NOT an alternative voting system.'[5] The fact that health and defence spending are linked in only the loosest possible way to the cost of changing a voting system was insignificant. On an issue that was hardly galvanising public debate, the No campaign tugged on the emotional heartstrings and won.

In the Brexit campaign, the media came in for some criticism of how they covered the row over the NHS figure. The Remainers argue that the broadcasters did not push back against it enough and consequently the figure both spread and gained credibility. The BBC's Rob Burley rejects this, pointing out that 'Reality Check [the BBC's fact-checking team] did push back on the credibility of the number on the side of the bus'. He says that 'the Remainers, the Leavers, they'll find evidence that they think is there for us not being impartial, for us pursuing one agenda or another', but again he gives such a claim little credence.

While there was plenty of good coverage discussing the claim's merits or lack thereof, one cannot help but feel that mainstream media could have done more to scrutinise it. Too often the images of the bus were shown without explanation, or politicians were allowed to make the claim unchallenged. The fact that it was clearly so effective will surely only encourage more falsehood in public debate, dragging it further into the mire.

MORE LEAVE LIES

Increased NHS funding was not the only lie told by Leave campaigners in the build-up to the referendum. Former UKIP

5. https://www.bbc.co.uk/news/uk-politics-12564879

leader Nigel Farage launched a poster from the Leave.EU campaign, another pro-Leave group but one that was not given official campaign status, showing a queue of people at a border accompanied with the caption 'Breaking Point – The EU has failed us all'.[6]

The poster's politics are ugly and divisive, using the kind of anti-immigrant rhetoric that lay at the heart of so much anti-EU messaging. In this case, it is also deeply misleading. The image used on the poster is of refugees on the Croatia–Slovenia border, not economic migrants trying to enter Britain from the EU. Farage was asked about this by journalists, but the poster is very direct, and the specifics were never made clear in a referendum campaign in which immigration was so high on the agenda. It is obvious that Leave.EU were using this poster to play on that fear.

Trying to justify the poster, Farage said:

'If you believe, as I have always believed, that we should open our hearts to genuine refugees, that's one thing. But, frankly, as you can see from this picture, most of the people coming are young males and, yes, they may be coming from countries that are not in a very happy state, they may be coming from places that are poorer than us, but the EU has made a fundamental error that risks the security of everybody.'

This statement disingenuously conflated the rise in refugees following the devastating civil war in Syria with economic migration, a key concern in many of the Brexit heartlands. Furthermore, Britain's commitments to refugees are not connected to its membership of the EU. But once again, the

6. https://www.theguardian.com/politics/2016/jun/16/nigel-farage-defends-ukip-breaking-point-poster-queue-of-migrants

specifics do not matter. It is the sentiment behind the poster – the emotion, not the reality – that really counts.

On a similar theme, the official Leave campaign claimed that Turkey's accession to the EU was imminent, and given Turkey's high birth rate, the consequence of this would be 'an additional million people added to the UK population from Turkey alone within eight years'.

The Leave campaign insisted that this imminent Turkish influence would also be a security risk, as 'crime is far higher in Turkey than the UK. Gun ownership is also more widespread.' They claimed that 'because of the EU's free movement laws, the government will not be able to exclude Turkish criminals from entering the UK'.

This was all endorsed by then defence minister and Leave supporter Penny Mordaunt, who went on to serve in Theresa May's cabinet, and was illustrated by another poster – this time showing an EU passport as a door with footsteps leading towards it and the slogan 'Turkey (population 76 million) is joining the EU'. The image also appeared on the official Leave campaign's Twitter account.[7] At the time, Mordaunt said: 'We are currently sending over £1bn to Turkey to help it to join the EU. We must recognise the huge strain this will place on our NHS as more people come here, without giving it any chance of planning for such increased demand'.[8] On the same day as those comments appeared in the *Observer*, she told Andrew Marr that it was 'very likely' that Turkey would join the EU.[9]

Indeed, Turkey was a fairly regular theme in the Leave campaign's social media output. It published a video on Facebook, juxtaposing David Cameron denying that Turkey

7. https://twitter.com/vote_leave/status/734664463757004800
8. https://www.theguardian.com/politics/2016/may/21/vote-leave-prejudice-turkey-eu-security-threat
9. https://www.youtube.com/watch?v=DxSz4levAxc

would join the EU and an outbreak of violence in the Turkish parliament. It also quoted the then prime minister saying he wanted 'to pave the road from Ankara to Brussels'. Note, Cameron is not explicitly saying he wants Turkey to join the EU. His comment could just as easily mean he wanted to improve diplomatic relations between the two.[10]

On 9 June, just two weeks before the vote, it tweeted an image of Michael Gove and the quote from him urging people to register to vote and warning that 'people will only have one chance to vote on whether they want to share free movement of people with Turkey'.[11]

(It also ignored the fact that Boris Johnson had at one point been quite open to the idea of Turkish accession to the EU.)

Again, this was all a total fabrication, looking to exploit nasty, racist instincts. Turkish attempts to join the EU had been going on for years in the run-up to the UK referendum and had showed no signs of significantly moving forwards, certainly not in the time frame implied by the Leave campaign. Indeed, in the months and years following the referendum it became even less likely they would succeed as Turkish president Recep Tayyip Erdoğan passed a new constitution, won re-election and lurched further into authoritarianism.

As Dr James Ker-Lindsay of the LSE wrote in 2018: 'Even if the country radically changed course, it seemed inconceivable that it could possibly join any time before 2030. And even if it did join, it would seem almost certain that the EU would institute a lengthy transitional control on freedom of movement.'[12]

10. https://www.facebook.com/voteleave/videos/turkey-population-76-million-is-joining-the-eu-our-schools-and-hospitals-already/604310329745895/

11. https://twitter.com/vote_leave/status/740836645109399552

12. http://blogs.lse.ac.uk/brexit/2018/02/08/did-the-unfounded-claim-that-turkey-was-about-to-join-the-eu-swing-the-referendum/

All in all, the claim that a million Turks were going to come to Britain really did not stack up.

Following the referendum, Michael Gove conceded to Tom Baldwin in an interview for the latter's book *Ctrl Alt Delete* that the Leave campaign had indeed appealed to 'some very low sentiments' over the issue of Turkish immigration and admitted that 'if it had been left entirely to me the Leave campaign would have had a slightly different feel'.[13]

That is easy to confess to after the event, but Ker-Lindsay argues that this lie may even have helped secure a victory for the Brexiteers:

'Ultimately, the claim that Turkey was on course to join the European Union, and that this would lead to an almost immediate surge of immigrants into Europe, and thus the United Kingdom, seems almost certain to have shaped the views of a significant number of voters. Whether this was merely an additional reason to leave – or was the issue that swung it – is hard to say. However, given the significance of the immigration debate and Turkey's central role in that discussion, and given how close the final result was, there is a good case to be made that the unfounded claims made by the Leave campaign about Turkish membership of the EU have ultimately cost Britain its own membership of the Union.'[14]

It is a huge claim from Ker-Lindsay and one that is obviously not possible to verify definitively. However, given how crucial immigration was in the Brexit debate, it certainly has substantial merit and demonstrates the power fake news can have in the context of political campaigns.

13. https://www.theguardian.com/politics/2018/jul/16/michael-gove-admits-leave-was-wrong-to-fuel-immigration-fears
14. http://blogs.lse.ac.uk/brexit/2018/02/08/did-the-unfounded-claim-that-turkey-was-about-to-join-the-eu-swing-the-referendum/

McGrory says the Remain campaign used data more responsibly: 'There's a number of reports out about basically what you get out of EU membership. There's one from a few years ago that says basically for every £1 we put in, we get £10 back in turn. That's not from the EU, that's in terms of economic growth, benefits of the single market and all the rest of it.'

While he concedes that figure is 'complex, contestable and open to scrutiny', he says it is by no means the highest estimate that has been put forward of the benefits Britain got from EU membership. However, the Remain campaign 'got scared off that because it came in for some criticism, including on the BBC from [politics presenter] Andrew Neil'. He laments this, saying: 'It's easily more justifiable than £350 million. It's independent people saying it.' He adds: 'I think we took a more responsible attitude towards it, we backed off.'

He recalls asking an audience of statisticians he was addressing after the campaign whether they thought the Leave or Remain campaign had used statistics more accurately. Only about two in the audience of 150-odd people put their hands up to say the Remain campaign had behaved worse, compared to 'most of the rest of the audience, well over 150 people' who said the same about Leave.

McGrory says this adds to his sense of frustration that both campaigns, and most people involved in politics, are tarred with the same brush, that nobody believes what they say. He feels that although his campaign worked hard to use peer-reviewed and accurate information, 'we were given zero credit for it. Zero credit by the media. Zero credit by the public.' He said that ultimately his conclusion from the campaign was not 'that you fight fire with honesty'.

There are then serious and legitimate criticisms of the Leave campaign – and an important point to be learned for campaigns in the future. In order to counter fake news, we first have to call it out for what it is. Reporters rightly will not feel it is their place to say who is, to put it crudely, 'good' or 'bad' during a political debate. It is not their job to do so. It is, though, absolutely their job to call out fact and fiction. False equivalence in which everybody is presented as equal, in which all the information has the same value, helps nobody.

While it may well be true that the Remain campaign was more responsible in how it presented its research and data, those on the Remain side are far from perfect. The lies were not as brazen, but the issues with the campaign contributed to the general negative feelings around the debate and a sense of mistrust amongst the public about what they were being told. The conspiracies have not stopped since the referendum result was declared, either...

REMOANERS

While the most egregious, and ultimately successful, bits of fake news were spread by the Leave campaign, it would not be fair to lay the entire blame at its door. In the months and years since the vote to leave the EU, high-profile figures like Andrew Adonis, a member of the House of Lords and former cabinet minister under Tony Blair, have indulged in conspiracy theories every bit as grand and convoluted as those of their opponents.

Adonis wrote to the BBC's director general Lord Tony Hall, demanding that the BBC's major politics presenter, Andrew Neil, be removed from his job because of his 'pro-Brexit bias'.[15] Neil, chairman of the UK's leading centre-right magazine, the *Spectator*, which backed Brexit,[16] may well himself be a

15. https://www.telegraph.co.uk/news/2017/09/04/brexiteer-unionist-hate-say-referendum-divisions-may-never-heal/
16. https://www.spectator.co.uk/2016/06/out-and-into-the-world-why-the-spectator-is-for-leave/

Eurosceptic. However, the claim this was influencing his broadcasting felt like a bizarre, partisan attack on a highly accomplished and experienced journalist who is known for not usually giving his subjects an easy ride.

Adonis has further claimed that the BBC, an institution that prides itself on neutrality and is legally instructed to maintain it, is promoting Brexit, referring to it as the 'Brexit Broadcasting Corporation'. In another letter to Lord Hall, sent in April 2018, he said that the BBC's editorial decision to no longer report on Brexit as 'the binary choice which faced the electorate in the referendum' but instead to '[examine] the Brexit negotiations and the impact of Brexit on the UK and the wider world' was 'in straightforward and serious breach of your Charter'. Adonis said that the decision was affecting the BBC's coverage of Brexit and that it had become 'fundamentally corrupted on Brexit because of your desire to conciliate the Government and pro-Brexit campaign on the fundamental issue of leaving the European Union'.[17] His evidence was the BBC's decision not to cover large anti-Brexit protests that had taken place two weeks before he wrote.

Blair's former spin doctor Alastair Campbell, who was intimately linked to the forty-five minute claim discussed in an earlier chapter, backed up Adonis on his blog. 'It is not the BBC's role to act as an echo chamber for a government. Sadly, on Brexit, that is what it is in the main doing right now,' he wrote.[18]

Campbell added a further air of conspiracy, writing: 'There are voices within the BBC, privately, saying so. They need to find a spine too. If they, either the ideological or the weak,

17. https://www.pressgazette.co.uk/bbc-confident-in-its-brexit-coverage-in-face-of-complaint-from-labour-peer-claiming-it-has-been-fundamentally-corrputed/
18. https://alastaircampbell.org/2018/04/if-the-bbc-think-their-supine-stance-on-brexit-will-save-them-from-the-hard-right-they-are-naive-in-the-extreme/

seriously think the hard right forces now pushing hardest for hard Brexit will protect and nourish the BBC once their work is done, they are naive in the extreme.'[19] He then echoed Adonis' criticism of the BBC's editorial decision on the amount of coverage they gave anti-Brexit protests.

Aside from the irony of Campbell – who took a notoriously tough approach in getting over the government's message he served to journalists – complaining about the BBC following the government's line, there is actually nothing wrong with senior public figures criticising the BBC's or anyone else's coverage. There is nothing wrong with senior public figures saying they want Brexit stopped. The problem here, I would argue, is that it is tied up in conspiracy and does not deal with the reality of the situation.

The line of attack ignores the fact that the government had been explicit in saying Brexit was happening in some form or another. It was therefore both a reasonable and a responsible position from a national broadcaster to report that, try to outline what was happening in the negotiations and explain what the policy implications of that might be, instead of endlessly rerunning the debate that had taken place during the campaign. As ever, there is a difference between 'news that is wrong or false' and 'news you don't like'.

The other Remain conspiracy involves Russian interference in the referendum. Some high-profile Remain supporters have insisted that the Russian state intervened to swing the vote in favour of Leave. The truth, as ever, is more complicated. It seems likely that Russia ran a disinformation campaign in the run-up to the vote. Oxford University's Samantha Bradshaw told me that 'there was quite a bit of automation and automating polarising messages'.

19. Ibid.

Indeed, in November 2017, *Wired* magazine reported that 'a coordinated network of Russian-based Twitter accounts spread racial hatred in an attempt to disrupt politics in the UK and Europe'. They found that 'a network of accounts posted pro- and anti-Brexit, anti-immigration and racist tweets around the EU referendum vote while also targeting posts in response to terrorist attacks across the continent'.[20] Whether or not it had a real, tangible effect on the result remains, at best, unclear.

The Remain side should also be criticised for the deeply politically motivated doom-and-gloom assessments made by former chancellor George Osborne in the lead-up to the referendum, alongside his promise of a so-called punishment budget if Leave won. Sharing a stage with his predecessor in the treasury, Labour's Lord Alistair Darling, Osborne said that voting to exit the EU would leave a black hole in the economy requiring significant tax rises and cuts to spending to fix.[21]

There can be little doubt that Brexit will put huge economic pressures on the UK – some of which was apparent in the immediate aftermath of the referendum. However, Osborne's warning was a manipulation of information presented by the Institute for Fiscal Studies (IFS) to promote his political cause. This was shown when, in a statement in response to the market volatility following the leave vote, Osborne spoke only of contingencies already in place, not an emergency budget.[22] With Osborne and David Cameron exiting from Downing Street in the wake of the vote, such a punishment budget never happened. It apparently had been little more than an empty political threat.

20. https://www.wired.co.uk/article/brexit-russia-influence-twitter-bots-internet-research-agency
21. https://www.bbc.co.uk/news/uk-politics-eu-referendum-36534192
22. https://www.gov.uk/government/speeches/statement-by-the-chancellor-following-the-eu-referendum

All the behaviour of both campaigns did was facilitate an atmosphere of mistrust, in which much of the general public did not believe the information they were being given.

LIES, DAMNED LIES, AND STATISTICS

The Brexit campaign is far from the only time statistics have been misused in public debate.

The aforementioned Sir Andrew Dilnot had cause to rebuke Iain Duncan Smith when he was the work and pensions secretary. In 2013 his department published a press release that included a quote from Duncan Smith in which he said: 'Already we've seen 8,000 people who would have been affected by the cap move into jobs. This clearly demonstrates that the cap is having the desired impact.'[23]

He was using statistics to back up his claim that one of his key policies – a cap on the level of benefits people can receive – was working. Pretty standard fare, right? Politician implements a policy, says it works. Hardly hold-the-front-page stuff.

Except the reality was not so simple. Nicola Smith of the Trades Union Congress wrote to the UK Statistics Authority about the release. The response to the complaint from Sir Andrew was devastating. He said the claim that there were 8,000 people in work thanks to the cap 'was unsupported by the official statistics'. That is about as damning as it gets from the usually mild-mannered Statistics Authority.

Sir Andrew also wrote to Duncan Smith and told him that the 'statistics [did] not comply fully with the principles of the Code of Practice, particularly in respect of accessibility to the sources of the data, information about the methodology and

23. https://www.theguardian.com/politics/2013/may/09/iain-duncan-smith-benefits-cap-statistics

quality of the statistics and the suggestion that the statistics were shared with the media in advance of their publication'.[24]

Duncan Smith refused to back down. He told Radio 4's *Today* programme, Britain's agenda-setting morning radio broadcast, that he had 'a belief I am right'. You would struggle to find a better example of post-truth politics in action. The facts were not in Duncan Smith's favour, but emotion was, so he stuck by his narrative anyway, deciding that instinct and sentiment were just as good as data.

In 2018 Sir Andrew's successor, Sir David Norgrove, wrote in similar terms to Education Secretary Damian Hinds. The issue centred on a claim made by Hinds at that year's Conservative Party conference that 1.9 million more pupils were studying in schools deemed 'good' or 'outstanding' by the inspectorate, Ofsted. Sir David promptly told Hinds that while the number was 'accurate as far as it goes, this figure does not give a full picture'.

The number was not exactly wrong, but it wasn't exactly right either.

In his letters, Sir David has eloquently and succinctly outlined the real issue of statistics in the post-truth era. It is not always that they are false, per se. It is that politicians are happily manipulating them until they are almost meaningless. Given the manner in which they are used – to support political positions – these examples certainly fall into the realm of fake news.

In that example about schools, Hinds and his colleagues brushed over crucial context for the figures – a significant increase in student numbers and increased gaps between Ofsted inspections of well-ranked schools.

---

24. https://www.statisticsauthority.gov.uk/archive/reports---correspondence/correspondence/letter-from-andrew-dilnot-to-rt-hon-iain-duncan-smith-mp-090513.pdf

There is so much information and data out there now that it is easy to blind people with statistics. The old cliché 'lies, damned lies, and statistics' has never felt more relevant. Politicians, in particular, can almost always find a data point that backs up their argument, totally degrading the public's trust in such information.

In that letter to Hinds, Sir David also complained that 'the UK Statistics Authority has had cause to publicly write to the Department with concerns on four occasions in the past year' and that 'I regret that the Department does not yet appear to have resolved issues with its use of statistics'. One might argue that this is because the education department was all too happy to keep pushing numbers that suited them, even if they were not statistically robust.

Sir Andrew and co-author Michael Blastland write in their book *The Tiger That Isn't*: 'Too many find it is easier to distrust numbers wholesale, affecting disdain, than to get to grips with them.'[25] Writers like Nate Silver and Philip Tetlock have tried to bring good use of statistics and understanding of probability to the masses, but politicians misusing data makes their task all the more difficult.

Sir Andrew and Blastland concede in their book that numbers cannot be perfect. However, when used correctly they are a vital tool for the public to understand public policy and its effects.

They can also provide crucial guidance to help us navigate the post-truth era. To have any hope of this, politicians and the media must stop misusing them.

Which brings us to the greatest abuser of truth of all…

25. Andrew Dilnot and Michael Blastland, *The Tiger That Isn't* (Profile Books, 2008), pp. 2–3.

7

Donald Trump: the post-truth president

While Brexit pushed post-truth politics to a new level, if any development truly typifies the era, it is the election of Donald Trump as the forty-fifth president of the United States. He is the personification of an unstable and untruthful time.

President Trump's lack of interest in the truth did not begin when he entered the political arena. He revelled in lying for years beforehand, seeming to take a bizarre glee in misleading people to get what he wants, to impress them or simply for his own personal amusement. He has no regard for the truth at all and never really has.

Details do not matter to President Trump – all accounts of his presidency depict a man who has no focus and little ability to concentrate. What is important is how you sell something, what the story is and if it gets you what you want. To put it simply, Donald Trump is the post-truth president.

Trump lies about everything, from the serious to the seemingly irrelevant. He would regularly brag to visitors at his Mar-a-Lago retreat in Florida that the tiles in his daughter

Ivanka's bedroom had been drawn by Walt Disney himself. They had not. According to the *New York Times*, when his butler showed his distaste at him repeating this lie, Trump would laugh and reply 'Who cares?'[1] It was a good story, why ruin it with the truth?

It was that same approach that President Trump applied to politics. Indeed, one of his first political interventions, his long insistence that President Barack Obama had not been born in America, was a lie. Obama was provably born in the state of Hawaii.

In a feature for *Politico Magazine*, journalist Maria Konnikova noted that, compared to other figures in public life, 'Donald Trump is in a different category' when it comes to lying, nothing that 'the sheer frequency, spontaneity and seeming irrelevance of his lies have no precedent'. She reported that people who had monitored Trump over a number of years said that the lying was 'an ingrained habit'. New York tabloid writers who reported on him during the 1980s and 1990s said the frequency and pointlessness of his lies were of a different order of magnitude to his contemporaries.[2] It is the pointlessness of the lies that is so telling – Trump lies simply for the sake of it.

Indeed, lying was such a feature of how Trump did business that Tony Schwartz, the ghostwriter of Trump's 1987 autobiography *The Art of the Deal*, had to come up with a phrase to describe it – 'truthful hyperbole'. It perfectly sums up his constant stream of exaggerations and lies. The future president apparently loved the phrase.[3]

1. https://www.nytimes.com/2016/03/16/us/politics/donald-trump-butler-mar-a-lago.html
2. https://www.politico.com/magazine/story/2017/01/donald-trump-lies-liar-effect-brain-214658
3. Ibid.

So ingrained into his personality is lying that Bob Woodward, in his book *Fear: Trump in the White House*, reports that economic advisor Gary Cohn had described the president to associates as 'a professional liar'.[4]

Given the office he has risen to, the mistruths now have real significance. Trump conducted an interview with *Time* magazine's Washington Bureau chief Michael Scherer in March 2017, two months into his presidency. The whole transcript provides a valuable insight into President Trump's psyche. What leaps out in particular, though, is Trump's total conviction that he is right or, at the very least, will ultimately be proved right at some undefined point in the future. If whatever he has claimed does not in fact transpire, that is no problem – it means someone else is at fault, i.e. he is actually right but other people ruined it.[5]

A central theme in the conversation between Scherer and Trump is the president's wild accusation that his predecessor, President Obama, wiretapped him while still in office.

At one point in the conversation, Trump quotes a news story from Politico that read: 'Members of the Donald Trump transition team, possibly including Trump himself, were under surveillance during the Obama administration following November's election. House intelligence chairman Devin Nunes told reporters…'

'Wow,' says President Trump, believing he is vindicated, 'Nunes said, so that means I'm right, Nunes said the surveillance appears to have been… incidental collection, that does not appear to have been related to concerns over Russia.'

Scherer tries to point out to the president that he is not right, that 'incidental collection would not be wiretapping of

4. Bob Woodward, *Fear* (Simon & Schuster, 2018), p. 338.
5. http://time.com/4710456/donald-trump-time-interview-truth-falsehood/

you' but would instead be the wiretapping of others. President Trump, though, is having none of it. He interrupts, saying: 'Who knows what it is? You know, why, because somebody says incidental.' The specifics did not matter one iota; all President Trump heard and saw was vindication.

Equally significant is how carefree he was in dismissing the idea that an institution, one now ultimately in service to him, might be telling the truth. President Trump revels in the institutional collapse that we discussed earlier – egged on in the campaign and the early days of his presidency by Steve Bannon.

In turns out the idea that he had been monitored by his predecessor had been something of an obsession for President Trump and his administration. As Michael Wolff documents in his explosive book *Fire and Fury*, Trump was convinced that Obama had spied on him. (Indeed, President Trump was actually convinced the whole US system was working to thwart him, according to Wolff.[6])

A *New York Times* story added fuel to the fire. It detailed the Obama administration's concerns that intelligence relating to the Trump campaign's links with Russia 'could be covered up or destroyed', which led to 'a push to preserve the intelligence that underscored the deep anxiety with which the White House and American intelligence agencies had come to view the threat from Moscow'.[7]

Wolff says that for Trump, encouraged by his press secretary at the time, Hope Hicks, this was all he needed to confirm interference and that the Obama administration had been working with the intelligence agencies to disrupt his presidency.

6. Michael Wolff, *Fire and Fury* (Little, Brown, 2018), pp. 158-160.
7. https://www.nytimes.com/2017/03/01/us/politics/obama-trump-russia-election-hacking.html

As Scherer was trying to point out, what had actually happened was that people associated with Trump had been picked up by incidental collection, during surveillance of other people. Still, the president was convinced otherwise, and early in the morning on 4 March 2017 he launched a Twitter tirade accusing Obama of 'having his wires tapped' and 'McCarthyism'.[8]

In a separate example, in that same interview with Scherer, Trump referred to his comments 'about Sweden' – President Trump had wrongly said there had been a terror incident in the Scandinavian country.

The president almost conceded he had been wrong, but insisted that 'the following day, two days later, they had a massive riot in Sweden, exactly what I was talking about, I was right about that'. He was trying to twist the truth to vindicate a false statement. Again, when the interviewer pointed out Trump's inconsistencies, he did not flinch, replying: 'No, I am saying I was right. I am talking about Sweden. I'm talking about what Sweden has done to themselves is very sad, that is what I am talking about.' Truthiness in action.

On yet another occasion, Cohn warned the president that Australian prime minister Malcolm Turnbull was likely to bring up a steel tariff exemption Trump had promised him at a previous G7 summit. Trump told Cohn that he was 'going to deny' having had the conversation with his fellow world leader, adding: 'I never had that conversation with him.'[9]

It goes on. During the 2018 midterm campaign, President Trump repeated the lie that the US stock exchange had opened the day after the 9/11 attacks – he was trying to justify hitting the campaign trail after a shooting at a Pittsburgh synagogue.

8. https://twitter.com/realdonaldtrump/status/837989835818287106?lang=en
9. Bob Woodward, *Fear* (Simon & Schuster, 2018), pp. 207–209.

He was also wrong. It had taken six days for the stock exchange to reopen after the attack.

The lies are, in fact, nearly constant. On 13 September 2018 the *Washington Post*, which records the president's claims in a database, said it had calculated that Trump had made over 5,000 false or misleading claims by that point in his presidency. It included him publicly making 125 such statements on one day alone (7 September 2018) – the highest recorded on a single day. The newspaper said he managed that in just two hours.

These lies are not just about ephemera. The newspaper found that Trump had made the false claim that the Russia investigation was made up or a hoax on almost 140 occasions. However, a declassified report on Russian efforts to sway the 2016 election revealed that security agencies had 'high confidence' their fears of meddling were correct.[10]

On a further 1,573 occasions, Trump made false or misleading statements about economic issues.

Those around the president indulge in fake news too. There was advisor Kellyanne Conway's infamous 'alternative facts' shortly after the inauguration. Then, in December 2018, Roger Stone, a former close confidant of President Trump, admitted he had used the InfoWars website to spread lies about Guo Wengui after the exiled Chinese businessman sued Stone.[11]

Far from the power of office mellowing him, President Trump's lying has escalated since his inauguration. That 5,000th false statement came on day 601 of his presidency, giving an average of 8.3 false or misleading claims a day. However, in the first 100 days of the presidency, the average was 4.9 claims per day.

10. https://www.washingtonpost.com/politics/2018/09/13/president-trump-has-made-more-than-false-or-misleading-claims/
11. https://www.wsj.com/articles/roger-stone-admits-spreading-lies-on-infowars-11545093097?mod=searchresults&page=1&pos=1

One could fill a whole book with the tales and lies President Trump has told. It would be instantly out of date. The lies happen on a daily basis. Far from counting against him, lying actually encourages President Trump's supporters.

LYING DEMAGOGUE

A study published in the February 2018 edition of the *American Sociological Review* by researchers from MIT and Carnegie Mellon University detailed an environment in which the truth is seen as the norm. President Trump's supporters want him to break these norms; things are flipped on their head to such an extent that his lying is not only tolerated by his supporters but fully embraced. It is part of the appeal.

The researchers explained that they took on the project because they were 'unaware of any research that explains why voters might see a "lying demagogue" – someone who deliberately makes evidently false statements and breaks publicly endorsed prescriptive norms while catering to widely held private prejudices – as authentic'.[12]

Trump fits the description of the lying demagogue perfectly. Despite living in a gold-covered Manhattan tower block named after him, he likes to tap into a disillusionment with the elite. (Wolff's book outlines that Trump is desperate to be accepted by the elite but has always felt somewhat belittled and sneered at by them.)

The research shows that those who voted for him actually like his lies because they mean his voters have more in common with the man they want to shake up the establishment. One of the researchers explained to CNN that even the most blatant

12. Oliver Hahl, Minjae Kim and Ezra W. Zuckerman Sivan, 'The Authentic Appeal of the Lying Demagogue: Proclaiming the Deeper Truth about Political Illegitimacy', *American Sociological Review*, 83 (1) (2018): 1–33.

lies told by Trump will resonate with his supporters because they feel they are touching on a much deeper truth than what is being discussed on the surface. Researcher Ezra Zuckerman Sivan said that this makes it 'much harder to defeat at some level, because I can justify almost anything under those terms and say, "Yeah, it's not the explicit things I say, it's what's implicit, a deeper truth"'.[13]

The report itself concludes that:

> 'insofar as Trump had no chance of being acceptable in elite eyes, this made him even more credible as an authentic champion of his supporters – mainly Americans who also felt disrespected by cultural elites. And it likely made his lying demagoguery even more credible. If the key to the authentic appeal of the lying demagogue is that he is signalling a willingness to be regarded as a pariah by the establishment, Trump was certainly a credible pariah. In this sense, his statements reminded his voters that he is a pariah just like them.'[14]

The kind of disconnect that this report illustrates was actually predicted decades earlier, by Seymour Lipset. Writing in the *American Political Science Review* in March 1959, Lipset said: 'A crisis of legitimacy is a crisis of change, and therefore its roots, as a factor affecting the stability of democratic systems, must be sought in the character of change in modern society.'[15]

As we have seen, such a crisis of legitimacy is indeed occurring, and Trump is using it to his advantage. His lies

13. https://edition.cnn.com/2018/05/05/politics/trumps-lies-authentic-to-his-supporters/index.html
14. Oliver Hahl, Minjae Kim and Ezra W. Zuckerman Sivan, 'The Authentic Appeal of the Lying Demagogue: Proclaiming the Deeper Truth about Political Illegitimacy', *American Sociological Review*, 83 (1) (2018).
15. Seymour Martin Lipset, 'Some Social Requisites of Democracy: Economic Development and Political Legitimacy', *The American Political Science Review*, 53 (1) (1959): 69-105.

make him a more authentic and empathetic character to his supporters. It is hard to think of an individual who better sums up the post-truth era.

THE MUELLER REPORT

On April 18, 2019 a heavily redacted version of the report by special counsel Robert Mueller on Russian interference in the 2016 US presidential election was made public. This followed months of speculation, uncontained by Attorney General William Barr releasing a summary of Mueller's findings weeks earlier.

The dense document, all 448 pages of it, tried to unpack what, if anything, had really happened between the Trump campaign and Russia. However, the future president and his associates' contact, or lack thereof, with figures in Russia is for other people to dissect. What is interesting in terms of this book is that the report laid bare how central mistruth is to Trump and those around him. It said that 'the investigation established that several individuals affiliated with the Trump Campaign lied to the [Special Counsel's] Office, and to Congress, about their interactions with Russian-affiliated individuals and related matters'.[16]

It further explained that 'those lies materially impaired the investigation of Russian election interference'. Formerly close advisers to President Trump – Paul Manafort and Michael Flynn – were both specifically named. Furthermore, 'former Trump organisation attorney Michael Cohen pleaded guilty to making false statements to congress' (in relation to a possible Trump Tower in Moscow).

This behaviour continued after details of the report were

---

16. https://www.justice.gov/storage/report.pdf

made public. Following the release of Attorney General William Barr's summary, President Trump said 'it was a complete and total exoneration'.[17]

He continued in a similar vein after the full, redacted, report was released. Trump tweeted that it found 'No Collusion with Russia (and No Obstruction). Pretty Amazing!' That message was echoed by Vice President Mike Pence, and Kellyanne Conway, who told reporters: 'What matters is what the Department of Justice and special counsel concluded here, which is no collusion, no obstruction, and complete exoneration, as the president says.'

Except that is not the case. The Mueller report specifically did not exonerate the president. Instead, it said: 'If we had confidence after a thorough investigation of the facts that the president clearly did not commit obstruction of justice, we would so state. Based on the facts and the applicable legal standards, however, we are unable to reach that judgment.'

Mueller's findings also said that 'while this report does not conclude that the president committed a crime, it also does not exonerate him'.[18] Barr included this information in his summary too.

Beyond the lies told by those connected to President Trump, the Mueller report laid out evidence of a Russian disinformation campaign. It found that Russia's Internet Research Agency (IRA) 'conducted social media operations targeted at large US audiences with the goal of sowing discord in the US political system'. It explained that these 'IRA operations included supporting the Trump campaign and disparaging candidate Hillary Clinton'. However, 'the investigation did not identify evidence that any US persons

17. https://www.nytimes.com/2019/03/24/us/politics/trump-exonerated.html
18. https://apnews.com/f75c4d5f001648e6bb6c2e33ff4eda77

knowingly or intentionally coordinated with the IRA's interference operation'.

The Mueller report outlines the staggering social media reach that the Russian organisation had. It included Instagram accounts with 'hundreds of thousands of US participants' and Twitter accounts with 'tens of thousands of followers, including multiple US political figures who retweeted IRA-created content'. These kinds of systems are able to spread fake news to huge swathes of the electorate at the click of a button. Furthermore, Mueller concluded that the IRA used Twitter to promote rallies it organised in support of Trump.

It will take years for us to really know everything that happened during the run-up to the 2016 US presidential elections. In all likelihood, we will never have a complete picture. However, the Mueller report clearly outlined a pattern of lying and fake news.

8

Fox in the hen house

It has become impossible to discuss our current media age without looking at one outlet in particular – an outlet that not only has redefined what news broadcasting looks and sounds like over the last two decades but in many ways now defines the post-truth era itself.

On 7 October 1996 Fox News was unleashed on America. There are, rightly, whole books dedicated to the story of how Fox News came to be and how it has grown. However, given how critical it is to the current media age, it is worth pausing at this juncture to specifically consider the outlet and its role in the post-truth era.

The station was a direct challenge by founders Rupert Murdoch and Roger Ailes to the rather dull fare they saw on US cable news at the time. It was also a response to what the two men considered the coastal, elite, liberal agenda of the existing news networks. Over the next twenty years, the station would grow to become the epicentre of politics on the right in America and would inspire a generation of media entrepreneurs trying to replicate its winning formula. Fox has moved beyond being a news network and become a cultural juggernaut. It dominates American politics in a way that its competitors such as CNN and MSNBC can only dream of.

Fox News does not follow conservative talking points. It writes them.

Politicians who follow the script are rewarded with supportive coverage and interviews beamed into millions of homes across the US. Those who do not face the full force of the channel's opposition or, worse, end up totally ignored. No Republican can hope to succeed without the support of Fox News. Few even bother to try. Trump is so in thrall to the channel, and in particular the programme *Fox and Friends*, that they have become a way of directly getting a message to the Oval Office.

Indeed, the 2016 US election that brought Trump to power was the moment the channel had been working towards for two decades. Although initially relatively hostile to Trump's candidacy, particularly after Trump clashed with star anchor Megyn Kelly, Fox undoubtedly played a key role in securing Donald Trump's remarkable ascent from New York reality TV star to commander-in-chief and president for rust-belt America. The channel ultimately gave Trump almost as much airtime as he could fill. With viewers flocking, the channel even allowed him to phone in to shows instead of being there in person.

FAIR AND BALANCED

From its inception until June 2017, Fox News' motto was 'fair and balanced'. The power and genius of this marketing slogan cannot be overlooked. It sits at the heart of what Fox News is and captures in three words why the station is so integral to the rise of the cynicism that led us to the post-truth era.

Michael M. Grynbaum summarised it perfectly in the *New York Times*: 'For conservative-leaning viewers, "Fair and Balanced" was a blunt signal that Fox News planned to counteract what Mr Ailes and many others viewed as a liberal bias ingrained in television coverage by establishment news networks.'[1]

Indeed, so central to the station was this motto that Fox News tried to sue Al Franken when in 2003 he titled his book *Lies and the Lying Liars Who Tell Them: A Fair and Balanced Look at the Right*. The company claimed 'fair and balanced' was a trademark. The case, it should be noted, failed, with Franken rejoicing that his opponent 'was literally laughed out of court'.[2]

With this tag line emblazoned across screens, Fox News pitched itself as being on the side of so-called ordinary Americans, as the truth teller fighting the good fight against its competitors. Extending the slogan to its logical conclusion means that those competitors were neither fair nor balanced and therefore should be not just ignored but mistrusted.

Crucially, the motto was always delivered with a knowing wink, a sideways glance that said, 'yes, we know we're biased. So are all the others. But at least we are on your side.' It is once again a sly dig from Murdoch and Ailes at their perceived enemy, the media elite they spent their careers trying to disrupt. What could wind up earnest J-school-trained hacks who worked at rival stations more than seeing a proudly conservative news outlet portraying itself as fair and balanced? What could irritate the viewers of such broadcasts more? It

1. https://www.nytimes.com/2017/06/14/business/media/fox-news-fair-and-balanced.html?mcubz=0&_r=0

2. https://www.the-tls.co.uk/articles/public/post-truth-sam-leith/

is the kind of pot-stirring that the alt-right and their media cheerleaders, some twenty years after Fox News first hit the airwaves, would take to its most extreme as they delighted in trolling opponents with internet memes and provocatively headlined websites.

Interestingly, in an interview, the channel's former left-wing contributor Sally Kohn told the *Women Rule* podcast that for a number of years Fox News was actually very sensitive to not explicitly pitching itself as a conservative station.[3] Such sensitivity seems to have long gone out the window.

Ailes, who died in 2017 shortly after leaving Fox News in a sexual harassment scandal, had long bought into the idea that mainstream media was biased and liberal. While there are legitimate criticisms to be made of outlets on both sides of the Atlantic for being too caught up in a London/New York/Washington bubble, pursuing this idea of bias helped Ailes in his attempts to discredit rival networks.

When President Richard Nixon's administration began discussing how to counter this perceived problem, Ailes put himself at the forefront of the conversation. He wrote extensive memos and pitched for lucrative contracts via his production company. One part of this was his idea to found the Capitol News Service, a big and brazen concept that involved transporting the clips the White House wanted to be used into local US television markets, bypassing the networks altogether. It never went ahead, but Ailes was a supporter, writing in a memo that he thought it was 'basically a very good idea'.

Despite having publicly positioned himself against such blatant propaganda in the past, when it came down to it Ailes was ultimately unconcerned about the ethics of a White

3. https://www.politico.com/story/2018/05/23/women-rule-podcast-sally-kohn-603283

House-run news outlet. Indeed, he made it clear that his production firm would bid to put it together.[4]

This is the confrontational philosophy that Ailes brought to Fox News, the thinking that lies behind its 'fair and balanced' tag line. It demonstrates a mindset that is obsessed with winning, both financially and politically, something that is crucial to the cable news outlet. It also has a profound cultural impact. If millions of people a day are watching Fox News and being told that it, and it alone, is the paragon of truth, that means legitimate news stories on other networks will be disbelieved and exaggerations or misrepresentations on Fox News will be taken at face value.

DIVIDE AND CONQUER

Under the leadership of Roger Ailes, Fox News became a media giant. It is hard to know quite what came first – Fox News or conservatives' mistrust of mainstream cable news networks. Either way, with a brilliant marketing slogan and meticulously planned production, Ailes exploited this growing mistrust to perfection. And profit.

Like a football team, Fox News encourages fanatical loyalty amongst its viewers. While it is not unheard of for people in the UK to categorise themselves as a '*Guardian* reader' or a '*Sun* reader', there is almost no other broadcast outlet in the world that is as central to its viewers' cultural and political identities as Fox News. This was apparent when the channel was engulfed in the sexual abuse scandal that ultimately saw Ailes removed – many Fox News fans believed Fox's political opponents were taking their favourite station down with baseless smears.

4. Gabriel Sherman, *The Loudest Voice in the Room* (Random House, 2017), pp. 72–74.

What often matters in a story broadcast on Fox News is the sentiment, not necessarily the reality, a key feature of the post-truth era. This stems from Ailes' long-term awareness of the power of visual narrative. Gabriel Sherman, in his essential biography of Ailes, describes how he developed a series of televised town halls for Richard Nixon's successful 1968 campaign for president. Ever the perfectionist, Ailes made sure everything from the panellists asking questions to the candidate's make-up to the stage lighting was as he wanted it. The broadcasts looked like real town halls, but the whole thing was designed to make Nixon look good.[5]

One incident in particular leaps out. A commentator called Jack McKinney questioned Nixon about a Marxist professor who had welcomed the victory of the Vietcong. McKinney, a print journalist, tried to make the case that there was a subtle but important difference between the professor welcoming the Vietcong's victory over US troops and calling for it. Live on television, Nixon did not have to negotiate the nuance; he could humiliate McKinney and savage the professor, essentially branding him a traitor. The power of the image designed by Ailes meant that Nixon was the patriot defending American troops, and everything else was abhorrent. There was no place, or need, for nuance.[6]

This is the style of programme that has helped Fox News become the commercial success it is. As with the Nixon debates, Ailes picked the winners. Panels may look like they are designed for balance, and left-wing commentators such as Sally Kohn have been given prominent voices on Fox News over the years,[7] but spend any significant amount of time

5. Ibid., pp. 45–58.
6. Ibid., pp. 54–55.
7. http://archives.cjr.org/feature/and_from_the_leftfox_news.php

watching the channel and you'll see that the conservative view always wins out. It is designed that way and has been from inception. Viewers are not getting a balanced demonstration of the arguments or issues and they are not meant to.

The programme *Hannity & Colmes* launched the career of now-superstar prime-time anchor Sean Hannity. Each episode of the programme was a debate between the right-wing Hannity and left-wing Alan Colmes. Interestingly, investigative reporter and liberal columnist Joe Conason auditioned for the role of Hannity's foil but was never asked back after a screen test; Patrick Halpin, who used to appear regularly on the programme, says that while the now-deceased Colmes was 'smart and knowledgeable', Conason 'would've been too strong for Hannity'.[8] The set-up was designed to make sure Hannity, and the viewpoint he represented, won out.

This is all a continuation of the divide-and-conquer approach Ailes employed when he was consulting for Republican candidates after the Nixon campaign. It was entirely deliberate and it was highly effective. For example, in 1970 Ailes was working on the senate campaign of Congressman Robert Taft Jr against the governor James Rhodes, who had pitched himself as the law-and-order candidate. Thirty seconds before a debate between the candidates was due to go live on television, Ailes strode up to Taft and handed him a note containing just one word: 'Kill'. He proudly went on to boast to a reporter that had 'shook up' his candidate.[9]

Ailes' aggressive approach to politics was conveyed across the channel he founded. He also always mixed politics and

8. https://www.nytimes.com/2017/11/28/magazine/how-far-will-sean-hannity-go.html?_r=0

9. Gabriel Sherman, *The Loudest Voice in the Room* (Random House, 2017), p. 69.

media in a way that was unique when he started but many have copied since.

MISINFORMATION MEANS POWER

In the course of building this megabrand, Fox News has been guilty of spreading huge amounts of misinformation, setting the tone for the post-truth era. Its line-up, particularly during commercially crucial prime-time hours, has delighted in giving a major platform to a variety of conspiracy theories. This includes numerous discussions of the shooting of a junior member of staff at the Democratic National Committee (DNC) called Seth Rich in the run-up to the 2016 presidential election.

Rich was murdered in the streets of Washington, DC, late one night, and at the time of writing there is no evidence that the incident was anything other than a robbery gone wrong, a tragic addition to the DC murder statistics. However, Hannity continued to push the agenda on television and radio that there was something more to the incident.

In fact, he alleged that Rich was murdered on the instructions of the Clintons. He claimed that Rich met with WikiLeaks, providing the whistleblowing site with the emails that so fatally undermined Hillary Clinton's campaign for the White House. The Clintons, the conspiracy goes, wanted to blame the Russians for the hack and so they had Rich killed.

There was no evidence of anything other than Rich being in the wrong place at the wrong time. This did not stop Hannity pushing the story, though. He kept trying to prove that it was Rich who was responsible for the leaks, not Russia acting on behalf of President Trump's campaign, of whom he is a vocal supporter.[10] He broadcasted persistently on the

10. https://www.nytimes.com/2017/11/28/magazine/how-far-will-sean-hannity-go.html?_r=0

young man's death. It was neither journalism nor political commentary. It was spreading a conspiracy theory for political reasons. However, because it made it onto Fox News, the issue seeped into the mainstream and became something that needed to be refuted and discussed.

In March 2018 Rich's parents sued Fox News. The lawsuit claimed that the network had taken the conspiracy theory 'from the fringe to the front pages and screens of the mainstream media'.[11] A piece of fake news had become front-page news.

Hannity pursued this while President Trump was under huge public pressure over his links with Russia. At the particular time Hannity was pushing conspiracies about Rich's death, the president was being heavily criticised for a story broken by the *Washington Post* that he had handed highly classified intelligence to Russian officials whom he had met with in the White House. Fox News broadly, and Hannity in particular, have appeared to completely downplay or ignore the significance of Trump's links with Russia.

Indeed, in August 2017 Rod Wheeler, the private investigator whose comments were used by Fox News to spark the conspiracy, filed a lawsuit alleging that the comments attributed to him were not his. The lawsuit said quotes in an article, which was later retracted, were 'fabricated'. Wheeler's legal representatives alleged that 'Fox News was working with the Trump administration to disseminate fake news in order to distract the public from Russia's alleged attempts to influence our Country's presidential election'.[12]

11. https://www.washingtonpost.com/news/morning-mix/wp/2018/03/14/fox-news-sued-by-parents-of-seth-rich-slain-dnc-staffer-for-conspiracy-theory-about-his-death/?utm_term=.09400a7a0206
12. http://variety.com/2017/tv/news/rod-wheeler-fox-news-seth-rich-sean-hannity-1202512081/

Tina Nguyen, writing for *Vanity Fair*'s Hive, describes a 'parallel universe' of conservative media. In this universe, the serious story of President Trump sharing highly classified intelligence with Russian officials during a White House meeting, published by the much-respected *Washington Post*, 'was a dud' instead of the major scoop it was rightly regarded as elsewhere.

The story was derided and ignored by Fox News and others within the conservative media orbit. Fox anchors discussed seemingly far more minor stories on air, such as incidents on college campuses, while the channel's website hid the story in tiny writing under the fold of its homepage. Nguyen explains: 'One chyron in the eight o'clock hour read simply "McMaster: *Washington Post* story on Russia meeting is false". The Fox News website buried the story entirely, hiding it well below the fold.'[13] Tucker Carlson's 8 p.m. show was not the only programme to pursue that editorial line. Either Fox has news editors with very little news sense, or the station was deliberately trying to hide the story for political reasons. It seems highly unlikely to be the former.

While media outlets should be praised for doing original work, not just following the perceived agenda of the day, neglecting to cover important issues, such as the president of the United States sharing classified information with a hostile foreign power, does the same damage as publishing made-up information. It distorts reality for the general public and means they are less well informed. It is a vital part of the post-truth media landscape, and Fox News is one of the major protagonists. Most potently of all, it has created a culture in

---

13. https://www.vanityfair.com/news/2017/05/trump-russia-leaks-conservative-news

which outlets can spin refusing to cover such stories as a virtue and claim it is their rivals who are not covering the real news.

Hannity, it is worth noting, is a regular confidant of Trump's; White House staffers have told the *Washington Post* that 'he basically has a desk in the place'.[14] The two men are in such regular contact, discussing talking points and policy issues, that some have referred to Hannity as a shadow chief of staff or shadow communications director.

INSIDE THE PARALLEL UNIVERSE

The 2016 election also marked something of a changing of the guard in American conservative media, with Fox News-inspired sites such as Breitbart coming into their own. Ailes, astute as ever, seemed to recognise this temporary power shift. As Michael Wolff put it in *Fire and Fury*: 'For thirty years, Ailes – until recently the single most powerful person in conservative politics – had humoured and tolerated Donald Trump, but in the end Bannon and Breitbart had elected him.'[15]

Key to Nguyen's 'parallel universe' are a number of outlets that have surfed the wake of Ailes and company and created a strong conservative media landscape. A landscape that has all too often spread rumour, conspiracy and falsehood.

The original of these is the Drudge Report. The grandfather of conservative media, Matt Drudge's news aggregation site launched in 1995, before even Fox News. The site shot to fame when Drudge broke, in his famous tiny type, that *Newsweek* magazine had chosen not to run a story about President Bill

14. https://www.washingtonpost.com/politics/hannitys-rising-role-in-trumps-world-he-basically-has-a-desk-in-the-place/2018/04/17/
e2483018-4260-11e8-8569-26fda6b404c7_story.html?utm_term=.e15a29c33ae6
15. Michael Wolff, *Fire and Fury* (Little, Brown, 2018), p. 2.

Clinton having an affair with a White House intern. Then he released her name, and neither his life nor Monica Lewinsky's was ever the same again.

Of course, that story was true. The affair was not fake news. However, Drudge's rise ushered in the media landscape discussed in this book.[16]

In the current version of the landscape, there are the big hitters, the likes of Breitbart and Infowars. Andrew Breitbart, who founded the network of websites, previously worked with Matt Drudge. In his autobiography, he wrote about how the two first met over the internet and how he 'had a tear running down [his] face'[17] as he read the Monica Lewinsky story on Drudge. He was convinced that what he calls the 'Democrat media complex' had tried to suppress the Lewinsky story and others.

In the same book, Breitbart describes mainstream journalists as 'partisan critical theory hacks who think they can destroy everything America stands for by standing on the sidelines and sniping at patriotic Americans'.[18]

Breitbart's site gained huge influence after his death, when its CEO Steve Bannon was appointed to jointly lead Donald Trump's campaign and then got a senior job in the White House.

Then there is Alex Jones. For decades, Jones worked to build a following on talk radio. He has pushed a variety of conspiracy theories, some of which, such as the aforementioned PizzaGate, have had serious real-world consequences.

The sickest of these was when he said that the Sandy Hook

16. https://www.theguardian.com/us-news/2018/jan/24/how-the-drudge-report-ushered-in-the-age-of-trump

17. Andrew Breitbart, *Righteous Indignation* (Grand Central Publishing, 2011), p. 56.

18. Ibid, p. 58.

school shooting was a fake, causing untold pain to the families of the victims. He repeatedly insinuated that the 2012 massacre was a 'giant hoax' perpetuated by those advocating for stricter gun-control laws in America. He claimed that the news coverage was faked, using a technical issue in a segment by CNN presenter Anderson Cooper to justify his point.

In April and May 2018 Jones was sued by some of the families of the students and teachers who were killed in the shooting, as well as a surviving FBI agent who responded. In one lawsuit, Jones was accused of being the 'chief amplifier for a group that has worked in concert to create and propagate loathsome, false narratives about the Sandy Hook shooting and its victims, and promote their harassment and abuse'.[19] In January 2019 Jones was told to hand over internal documents pertaining to the case to victims' families.[20] Then, a month later, Jones was ordered to submit sworn testimony on the case. He denied allegations throughout the proceedings.[21]

A report on NBC by Megyn Kelly in June 2017 also found examples of Trump repeating talking points originally broadcast by Jones.[22] Ian Collins has had Alex Jones appear on previous iterations of his radio programme. While he thinks Jones, and others such as David Icke, are 'fantastic' for bringing in listeners and lighting up a switchboard, he is clear that you 'mustn't take it that seriously'. However, he concedes that other 'people do' take what Jones says at face value. He notes that in court proceedings Jones' wife 'suggested he was a nutter and you've only got to look at his shows to see that'. However, he is a nutter with a powerful voice. Collins, like many other

19. https://edition.cnn.com/2018/05/23/us/alex-jones-sandy-hook-suit/index.html
20. https://www.nytimes.com/2019/01/12/us/alex-jones-infowars-lawsuit.html
21. https://edition.cnn.com/2019/02/14/us/alex-jones-sandy-hook-lawsuit/index.html
22. https://www.youtube.com/watch?v=-HzOqZeX3Yk&index=6&list=WL&t=0s

popular presenters, also knows he has a responsibility in whom he gives a platform to.

There are other sites in the hyperpartisan conservative media ecosystem too. Take the Daily Caller, the Washington Free Beacon and the Blaze, to name but a few, along with more sinister neo-Nazi sites such as the Daily Stormer.

Fox News, Drudge and those that have followed in their wake have created a febrile environment, convincing others that the media are not telling the truth or are suppressing stories, normally in cahoots with these outlets' political opponents. While they are all commercial rivals vying for eyeballs and advertising income, they have developed an ecosystem in which a shared political narrative is developed. They frequently cite each other's reporting, which has the effect of building a narrative for those who tune in only to the right-wing media bubble. It makes it easy to dismiss news and views coming from the outside, allowing the alternative narrative to take hold amongst a large number of people.

The coverage of the Russian intelligence leak is a perfect example of this ecosystem at work. Breitbart focussed on the supposed scandal of the information being leaked, claiming that it was the 'deep state' working against the president it supports. Then the Drudge report linked to Breitbart's piece, and its founder Matt Drudge claimed that the *Washington Post* was attacking Trump to support the interests of its owner, Amazon founder Jeff Bezos.[23] The circle was complete.

It is not just in the US that such an ecosystem is developing. BuzzFeed News reporter Miriam Berger outlines a similar phenomenon in Israel. She has reported on the growth of Channel 20, which is financed by Trump-supporting businessman Sheldon Adelson and operates on a similarly

23. Ibid.

partisan basis to Fox News. Berger says that 'Channel 20 grew out of the anti-leftist politics championed by Prime Minister Benjamin Netanyahu and thrives off a kind of symbiotic relationship with him and his more extreme-right competitors.'[24]

In the Israeli ecosystem, there is also the Adelson-owned freesheet *Israel Hayom*, which has dramatically shaken up the Israeli media market by being a free and widely available alternative to existing publications, and Arutz Sheva, a media network founded by members of the settler movement.

Netanyahu, it is worth noting, has taken a very Trump-like pleasure in baiting the media and successfully sued Israeli journalist Igal Sarna in June 2017. Like Trump with Fox, Netanyahu has also claimed that he can only fairly get his thoughts out on the partisan Channel 20.

Not all such outlets and ecosystems publish fake news themselves (although plenty do), but together they create the hyperpartisan media landscape that gives so much power to genuinely fake news when it emerges.

24. https://www.buzzfeednews.com/article/miriamberger/the-rise-and-rise-and-rise-of-israels-right-wing-media

9

Antisemitism: the original fake news

The eminent historian Deborah Lipstadt recalls the incredulity with which her refusal to appear on television with a Holocaust denier was met by the producer trying to book her. 'She found it hard to believe that I was turning down the opportunity to appear on her nationally televised show,' writes Lipstadt at the start of her book *Denying the Holocaust*. Professor Lipstadt explains that far from this being a one-off, she always rejects such requests. She says that her refusal 'is inevitably met by producers with some variation of the following challenge: Shouldn't we hear their *ideas, opinion,* or *point of view?*' Her contention, rightly, is that there is no point of view on the Holocaust, simply fact and (antisemitic) fiction.[1]

It should not require repeating, but we know that 6 million Jews were murdered during the Holocaust, alongside those from other targeted minorities such as homosexuals, Gypsies and communists. We know that gas chambers at Nazi

1. Deborah Lipstadt, *Denying the Holocaust* (Penguin Books, 1993), p. 1–2.

concentration camps were one of the key ways this horror was enacted. These are not points of view to be contested. These are proven, documented facts. Claiming otherwise, pretending that there is an alternative view that is being suppressed, is not only antisemitic and vile but simply untrue.

However, in 2000, Lipstadt and her publisher Penguin Books were sued by the historian David Irving, who was angry his Holocaust denial had led to Lipstadt branding him an antisemite. Irving lost in a landmark court case (later depicted in the film *Denial*).[2] Famously, the truth prevailed on this occasion, and Lipstadt won.

The academic David Hirsh, a senior lecturer in sociology at Goldsmiths University in London who has written extensively about left-wing antisemitism, said in an interview that 'Irving was busy trying to portray himself as the victim of the Jews and the victim of the publishers and the victim of Lipstadt and [Lipstadt's lawyer Anthony] Julius, the big Jewish lawyer'. He was invoking antisemitic memes even as he tried to use the courts to free himself from the label of Holocaust denier. He represented himself in court and tried to distort the situation and portray himself as the victim, even though he had brought the case.

Lipstadt may have won on this occasion, but victory for the truth is far from guaranteed. Even in Lipstadt's case, things were not as clear cut as they might have been. Hirsh explained that while the case 'was about things all good people agree on … people started writing articles saying, is the courts really the best place to have a history seminar? Should the courts be saying what's true and what isn't?'

No. They should not. I would argue that the issue here was not a history seminar being carried out in court. It was the fact that Lipstadt had described Irving as a Holocaust denier

2. https://www.theguardian.com/books/2000/apr/11/irving.uk

and he considered this libellous. The courts disagreed with him. Yes, to prove there was no libel Lipstadt's legal team had to demonstrate the falsity of Irving's claims and the veracity of information about concentration camps and the Holocaust. However, this is arguably more down to the quirks of the British legal system than anything else.

Irving was not alone in his use of pseudo-academia to promote a type of antisemitism that boils down to little more than racist conspiracy theory. In *The Case for Israel*, legal scholar and Israel advocate Alan Dershowitz highlights the case of Robert Faurisson and Noam Chomsky. Faurisson, a lecturer in French literature, wrote a book based on his insistence that the Holocaust was 'a massive lie'. He also claimed that Anne Frank's *The Diary of a Young Girl* was a forgery. This would be bad enough, but as a row over academic freedom broke out, Noam Chomsky came to Faurisson's defence. He allowed an essay of his to be used as a foreword to Faurisson's book and claimed that the assertions about the Holocaust were based on 'extensive historical research'. In reality, this was far from the case.[3]

Antisemitic propaganda is not new. Hatred of Jews based on conspiracy and falsehood goes back centuries, in fact, to when the Romans sought to establish Christianity as the sole religion, replacing Judaism. In the fourteenth century, as the bubonic plague ran riot, the scared public blamed the Jews for its spread based on the falsehoods that many already believed.

Later, in 1545, Martin Luther, the founder of Protestantism, published a treatise called *On the Jews and Their Lies*, which included the claim that Jews thirsted for Christian blood and should be killed.[4] Martin Luther told Christians to 'guard against the Jews,

3. Alan Dershowitz, *The Case for Israel* (Wiley, 2003), pp. 212-213.
4. https://www.adl.org/sites/default/files/documents/assets/pdf/education-outreach/Brief-History-on-Anti-Semitism-A.pdf

knowing that wherever they have their synagogues, nothing is found but a den of devils in which sheer selfglory, conceit, lies, blasphemy and defaming of God and men are practiced most maliciously and veheming his eyes on them'.

He went on to say that Jews 'are nothing but thieves and robbers who daily eat no morsel and wear no thread of clothing which they have not stolen and pilfered from us by means of their accursed usury'. Such antisemitic lies and tropes exist to this day.

The Nazis deployed ever more poisonous propaganda during the 1930s, including reprinting the Martin Luther document, to create a backlash against Jews based on these tropes and conspiracy theories. Professor David Welch explained for the BBC that 'the Jewish stereotypes shown in such propaganda served to reinforce anxieties about modern developments in political and economic life, without bothering to question the reality of the Jewish role in German society'.[5]

Maintaining that there will be £350 million more a week to spend on the NHS if Britain leaves the EU or that Hillary Clinton is seriously ill clearly pales into insignificance when compared to propaganda that led to the genocide of 6 million members of a particular religion. However, at its root, this all has the same contempt for the truth, the same malice aimed at the 'other'.

It should be no surprise, then, that time and time again, classic antisemitic imagery reappears in modern fake news. The perfect example is the Leave.EU poster discussed earlier that showed refugees on the Croatia/Slovenia border accompanied by the 'breaking point' slogan. It bore a frightening resemblance to a Nazi propaganda film that showed Eastern

5. http://www.bbc.co.uk/history/worldwars/wwtwo/
nazi_propaganda_gallery_05.shtml

European Jews queuing at borders and described them as 'parasites undermining their host countries'.[6]

Lest readers fear I am just lazily invoking Godwin's law (which states: 'as an online discussion continues, the probability of a reference or comparison to Hitler or Nazis approaches one') by conflating modern post-truth and Nazism for rhetorical or hyperbolic reasons, a leading chronicler of Hitler has outlined in significant detail the similarities. Ron Rosenbaum, author of *Explaining Hitler*, wrote in the *Los Angeles Review of Books* in February 2017:

'Few took Hitler seriously, and before anyone knew it, he had gathered up the nations of Europe like playing cards. Cut to the [US presidential election in 2016]. We had heard allegations that Trump kept Hitler's speeches by his bedside, but somehow we normalised that. We didn't take him seriously because of all the outrageous, clownish acts and gaffes we thought would cause him to drop out of the race. Except these gaffes were designed to distract. This was his secret strategy, the essence of his success – you can't take a stand against Trump because you don't know where Trump is standing.'[7]

Then, in the wake of the riots in Charlottesville in which far-right activists took to the street, Mike Godwin, the man whose name the law bears, declared himself happy for those responsible for the violence and murder of a counter-protestor to be branded Nazis, tweeting: 'By all means, compare these shitheads to Nazis. Again and again. I'm with you.'[8]

6. James Ball, *Post-Truth* (Biteback, 2017), p. 56.
7. https://lareviewofbooks.org/article/normalization-lesson-munich-post/
8. https://twitter.com/sfmnemonic/status/896884949634232320

THE LYING PRESS

Donald Trump and his supporters have found themselves embroiled in issues of antisemitism. Trump's relationship with antisemites is as questionable as his relationship with the truth.

Indeed, in October 2016, Buzzfeed News reporter Rosie Gray heard alt-right supporters of Donald Trump shouting the phrase 'Lügenpresse' towards the journalists gathered to cover the event. The word means 'lying press'. It was first used by a German author called Reinhold Anton during the First World War in reference to 'enemy propaganda', before being taken on by the Nazis to undermine and discredit the media.[9]

Gray reported that alt-right websites such as Occidental Dissent use the phrase regularly, as do alt-right Twitter accounts. When she confronted white nationalist leader Richard Spencer about this he was unconcerned. He told Gray that the phrase was 'all over the place'. 'It's typical alt-right,' Spencer explained. 'Serious... ironic... and with a sly reference to boot.'[10]

That 'sly reference', let us be clear, is to the Nazis.

The fact is that comparisons of the rhetoric, the distraction techniques and the lies of the current US president to Hitler are uncomfortably easy to make for a reason. Indeed, when I visited the Yad Vashem Holocaust memorial in Israel, my tour guide made a knowing reference to Hitler trying to 'make Germany great again'. Trump, like Hitler and other authoritarian or fascist leaders, has distorted the truth so the extraordinary is now the normal.

Perhaps unsurprisingly, this Nazi-inspired language has

9. https://www.haaretz.com/us-news/the-ominous-nazi-era-precedent-to-trump-s-fake-news-attacks-1.5438960
10. https://www.buzzfeednews.com/article/rosiegray/the-alt-right-has-adopted-an-old-nazi-term-for-reporters

made it to the UK as part of the Brexit debate. As a crunch parliamentary vote on Prime Minister Theresa May's proposed Withdrawal Agreement with the EU approached, a pro-Brexit march took place in London. The *Financial Times* writer Sebastian Payne noted one protestor had a sign with the word 'Lügenpresse' emblazoned on it.[11]

Hitler, it seems, invented the post-truth playbook long before we knew what it was.

THE ORIGINAL SIN

The political upheaval of 2016 may have been what made people take the issues of post-truth society seriously, but the long history of Holocaust denial and antisemitism shows that they are far from new. In many ways, they are the original fake news. Holocaust denial has been around for decades and antisemitism for centuries, spurred on by vicious propaganda that sits alongside the worst examples of fake news today.

Hirsh highlights that the notion of the all-powerful Jew that sits at the heart of much antisemitism 'requires conspiracy'. He gives the modern example of Jewish power in Hollywood, telling me that 'the charge is not that one particular Hollywood Jew, Steven Spielberg or whatever, does this or that' but that whatever crime is being committed is being committed by 'Jews in Hollywood' as a collective. There is always a conspiracy.

This original form of fake news holds strong to this day. In the summer of 2017, Hungarian prime minister Viktor Orbán launched a campaign against the Hungarian–American financier George Soros, using antisemitic memes to claim that the billionaire was unduly influencing Hungary's politics. The

---

11. https://twitter.com/SebastianEPayne/status/1071760136191045633

campaign portrayed Soros as a puppeteer controlling the country. Eight million Hungarian citizens were sent a survey asking if they agreed with a pro-migrant plan Soros was alleged to be supporting.

In a rebuttal statement, Soros hit back:

'On October 9, 2017, the Hungarian government mailed a national consultation to all 8 million eligible Hungarian voters purporting to solicit their opinions about a so-called "Soros Plan". The statements in the national consultation contain distortions and outright lies that deliberately mislead Hungarians about George Soros's views on migrants and refugees. Hungarian government officials also falsely claim that George Soros is somehow controlling the European Union decision-making process. In fact, decisions on how to address the migration crisis are made by EU member states and institutions, including the Hungarian government.'[12]

He also called out specific claims in the survey as lies. Heather Grabbe, director of the Open Society European Policy Institute, part of Soros's Open Society Foundation, told the *Guardian*: 'He's a very useful punching bag, because he's both the insider and the outsider, the meddling foreigner and the Hungarian Jew.'[13]

It is a perfect example of the so-called Jewish question – the prevailing idea that Jews do not really fit in anywhere. Hirsh says that work by Robert Fine and Philip Spencer indicates the fake news at the heart of this concept, in which the real issue is flipped on its head. 'The Jewish question is always fake news because the Jewish question is always an antisemitism question,' he says. 'The question is always "how do we solve

12. https://www.georgesoros.com/rebuttal/
13. https://www.theguardian.com/world/2017/jun/22/hungary-viktor-orban-george-soros

the problem of the Jews?" The real question is, how do we solve the problem of the antisemites?'

LEFT TURN

Hirsh has also written extensively on left-wing antisemitism. He explained to me that 'people on the left have been doing it for ten, fifteen, twenty years. People on the little dusty corners of the left have been doing it for longer. And it was we on the left who took it into the mainstream.' With the ascent of Jeremy Corbyn to the leadership of the Labour Party, left-wing antisemitism became a full-blown crisis. There are a variety of incidents and issues concerned with this that require unpacking. Some relate to what is known as antisemitic anti-Zionism, in which the perpetrator seeks to hide antisemitism behind criticism of Israel. Others are just fully fledged conspiratorial antisemitism, in a more traditional vein.

First, Corbyn ally Ken Livingstone was involved in a huge row over antisemitism in the summer of 2016 for repeatedly asserting that Adolf Hitler 'was supporting Zionism before he went mad and ended up killing 6 million Jews'.[14] Indeed, Hirsh has coined what he calls the Livingstone Formulation in honour of the former mayor of London. In his book *Contemporary Left Antisemitism*, he explains that 'the Livingstone Formulation conflates everything – criticism of Israel but also other things which do not seem to be so legitimate'.[15] He cites as a prime example how Livingstone compared a Jewish newspaper reporter to a concentration camp guard before pivoting to attack the government of Israel when he was criticised for doing so.

14. https://www.bbc.co.uk/news/uk-politics-44196298
15. David Hirsh, *Contemporary Left Antisemitism* (Routledge, 2017), pp. 28-29.

Like Irving, Livingstone tries to portray himself as the victim in these incidents. In his biography, he recalls that episode. Unrepentant, he remembers weeks of clashes as a whipped-up media row in which countless people, including his future mayoral rival Boris Johnson, supported him and urged him not to apologise. He even claims that 'the phrases "behaving like a concentration camp guard" and "jumped-up little Hitler" are common jibes in Britain' and that 'no journalist had ever complained before'.[16]

Things took a turn for the worse in 2018. In March of that year it emerged that Corbyn had been reported to be a member of and active in a number of Facebook groups in which antisemitism and Holocaust denial were rife. He was also found to have supported a mural that had clear antisemitic imagery in it. Then came a very weak statement of apology from Corbyn, in which he insisted on his 'total commitment to excising pockets of antisemitism that exist in and around our party' and insisted he'd never noticed the antisemitism in the mural, having only glanced at it quickly. Not surprisingly, this fell far short of what communal leaders felt was required, and they continued with their planned protest in Parliament Square, which attracted 1,500 people.

At every juncture, supporters of Corbyn insisted there was no problem and, crucially, that it was all a conspiracy cooked up by powerful Jews to try to dethrone their glorious leader. Indeed, there was even a counter-protest in Parliament Square by a fringe group called Jewish Voice for Labour, and some 2,000 Corbyn fans showed their support in an open letter to Corbyn, published on Facebook, that said he was facing the 'full onslaught of a very powerful special interest group mobilising its apparent, immense strength against

16. Ken Livingstone, *You Can't Say That* (Faber & Faber, 2012), pp. 514–517.

you'.[17] Whether the person who published this letter invoked this antisemitic meme deliberately is not clear. But when combined with the fact that the author also commented that the demonstration had 'employ[ed] the full might of the BBC' it becomes very apparent how central conspiracy is to the modern left and how easily that slips into antisemitism.

The lines in antisemitic anti-Zionism are somewhat more blurred. 'People always say, "where's the border between antisemitism and anti-Zionism?",' says Hirsh, 'and I always say, "well, I don't know," because you could have an antisemitic narrative which is made up entirely of non-antisemitic elements. Just like if you covered the front page of your newspaper every day with stories of black street crime… each story can be completely true and completely valid, but they create a racist narrative.'

17. https://www.independent.co.uk/news/uk/politics/jeremy-corbyn-labour-antisemitism-protest-powerful-special-interest-group-jewish-a8278761.html

10

Anti-vax, anti-truth

There is one final area of modern public policy that has been subjected to fake news, causing the most horrific of consequences, putting lives at risk and putting legitimate firms out of business.

Over the decades there has been a variety of scandals and public outcries over effects suffered by children allegedly as a result of vaccines they had recently received. Consequently, the anti-vaccine movement has grown in both the UK and the US and become a hugely powerful political voice. It plays on emotion – who could argue with grieving and despairing parents? Who could contest the images of suffering children? The movement often attempts to justify this emotion with (bad) science.

Unlike many of the other groups involved in spreading conspiracy theories and fake news, those who push an anti-vax agenda include both experts and non-experts, specialists and non-specialists. There have been high-level doctors who have infamously spread false information about vaccines, and they have then been backed by people who are not medical experts, including celebrities.

Some of the original anti-vax protests focussed on specific vaccines – whooping cough and later measles, mumps and rubella (MMR), for instance. However, it has morphed into a general movement opposing all vaccination and advocating so-called 'natural living', and is all too often based on bad data and questionable research. The media has to take some blame too, having hyped up cases and helped scare parents into not immunising their children.

The internet has, not surprisingly, proved to be the perfect breeding ground for these scare stories and misinformation. Websites such as naturalnews.com, vaccineimpact.com and mercola.com, alongside social media platforms, spread the anti-vax message. The websites display warnings and fears about all sorts of vaccines, such as the vaccineimpact.com headline that blared: 'Parents, Scientists and Doctors from Around the World Gather to Discuss How to Handle Increasing HPV Vaccine Injuries'. (The vaccine in question is the one offered to women to help prevent cervical cancer.) That post, from October 2018, said: 'The Ireland Government HSE (Health Service Executive) was invited to send representatives to attend, but they refused the opportunity to speak or listen to the world-renowned experts who attended.'[1] There are YouTube channels filled with dramatic, emotional anti-vax testimony.

Such headlines are a perfect indication of how anti-vaxxers use so-called experts to push their agenda – they keep the conspiratorial element of their fake-news-spreading peers, but instead of dismissing all experts, they seek to deploy their own.

A December 2017 article by Dr Mercola on his mercola.com

1. http://vaccineimpact.com/2018/parents-scientists-and-doctors-from-around-the-world-gather-to-discuss-how-to-handle-increasing-hpv-vaccine-injuries/

website asks: 'How Much Do You Really Know About Vaccine Safety?'[2] It shares scare stories and wild statistics about the illnesses suffered by children as a result of vaccination. It is compelling and looks scientific. That one article, from December 2017, has been shared at least 1,600 times.

The movement has also received high-profile backing. For example, Kat Von D, a tattooist and make-up entrepreneur with a huge social following, declared in June 2018 that her son would not be vaccinated. While some criticised her decision, her large online presence meant she received plenty of support too, and the anti-vax arguments were furthered by her advocacy.[3]

In his book *Deadly Choices*, author Paul Offit notes that 'many [parents] question all vaccines; and some, the integrity of those who gave them'. This is vital in understanding the anti-vax movement of the post-truth era. It is not just about people taking medical decisions on behalf of themselves or their children; it is often portrayed as a reaction to an elite conspiracy.[4]

Vaccines are not perfect. At one point a very small number of children were contracting and even dying from polio as a result of the polio vaccine. However, the anti-vax movement does not want to help make vaccines safer; it wants to stop them. The consequences have been deadly, reducing the overall level of immunisation, threatening the return of previously eradicated diseases and putting some of the most vulnerable people in society at risk.

One of the first instances of fake news around vaccines took place in the UK, on 26 October 1973, when well-regarded

2. https://articles.mercola.com/sites/articles/archive/2017/12/16/how-much-do-you-know-about-vaccine-safety.aspx
3. https://www.bbc.co.uk/news/world-us-canada-44483000
4. Paul A. Offit, *Deadly Choices* (Basic Books, 2010).

paediatric neurologist John Wilson told a meeting at the Royal Society of Medicine: 'Between January 1961 and December 1972, approximately fifty children have been seen at the Hospital for Sick Children in London thought to be due to the DTP inoculation.'

He was speaking of the combined vaccine against diphtheria, pertussis (better known as whooping cough) and tetanus. It was the pertussis component at the centre of the furore, with claims it was causing epilepsy, paralysis and mental disability.

Wilson's statements were the most mainstream articulation of fears put forward by other medical practitioners across Europe and the US. Mere months after sounding his warning, Wilson would appear on a prime-time television special for *This Week*, reiterating that he was convinced the pertussis vaccine could permanently damage children who received it.

The fallout was dramatic, with newspapers running ever more emotive headlines. Even medical professionals joined in the criticism, warning against immunisation. Consequently, the number of children being immunised fell off rapidly. So rapidly, in fact, that when James Cherry, a world-leading expert on whooping cough, was asked by the government to conduct a definitive study on the vaccine in 1997, he found that the illness had killed 600 children – significantly more than the original estimates.

The fears over DTP also crossed the pond to the US. On 19 April 1982 a Washington news channel aired an hour-long documentary titled *DPT: Vaccine Roulette*. The attention-grabbing film was broadcast multiple times and showed children damaged and disabled, allegedly as a result of the vaccine. The language used by reporter Lea Thompson was dramatic and could have been taken right out of the post-truth playbook. At the start of the film, she says that her reporting had found 'serious questions about the safety and effectiveness of the shot'. She adds that the 'overriding policy of the medical establishment has been to aggressively promote the use of the vaccine, but it has been anything but aggressive in dealing with the consequences'.

Medical experts were deployed in the film, and it prompted a major congressional response. Crucially, the fake news in the documentary caused such outcry and anguish amongst parents that a group of them came together to form what would become a highly powerful anti-vax lobbying group.

One of its most prominent members was Barbara Loe Fisher. Her son had suffered severe mental impairment hours after having the DTP vaccines. After watching *Vaccine Roulette*, Fisher joined up with other parents to create an anti-vax body called Dissatisfied Parents Together, which she led. Fisher had a major media presence and railed against almost every vaccine proposed.

Some years after Fisher's rise to fame, in 1994, Heather Whitestone was crowned Miss America. Deaf since the age of eighteen months, she was the first woman suffering from a severe disability to receive the accolade. Her mother told a local news reporter that the disability suffered by her victorious daughter had been caused by the DTP vaccine.

Not surprisingly, Fisher, who had written the book *Shots in the Dark: Why the P in the DPT Vaccination May Be Hazardous to Your Child's Health*, publicly gave her view on the case. She complained: 'It's so often that the parent who is with the child and witnesses the high fever, witnesses the convulsions, the shock or whatever – it comes down to whether the doctor agrees it was due to the vaccination just given.'

Making sure to inject a healthy dose of conspiracy into the proceedings, Fisher added that the medical community 'continues to try and sweep these children under the rug'.

The thing was, despite the insistence of Whitestone's mother, this high-profile case had nothing to do with DTP. Whitestone's local paediatrician made it publicly known that her deafness had in fact been caused by suffering from HIB meningitis as a child. The terrible irony of all this? Fisher had caused substantial concern about the HIB vaccine, appearing on national television in 1987 alongside a doctor and inaccurately claiming it caused diabetes.

Ultimately, there was such a rejection of the DTP vaccine that its price went up and a number of the firms producing it were eventually put out of business, leading to a chronic shortage.[5]

The row over DTP continues years after the concerns have been countered. The aforementioned 2017 Mercola article, for instance, asserts: 'DTP vaccine was associated with fivefold higher mortality than being unvaccinated.' According to the authors: 'All currently available evidence suggests that DTP vaccine may kill more children from other causes than it saves from diphtheria, tetanus or pertussis.'[6]

The basic biology behind brain damage eliminates any possibility that the pertussis vaccine could cause brain damage. Whooping cough can – the severe coughing it brings about can limit oxygen to the brain – but the vaccine is made from dead cells and does not cause coughing or brain damage. Other scientific studies rule out further possible ways the vaccine could cause damage, and over a number of years, various studies would also find no link between the DTP vaccine and various alleged side effects. This includes one in 2001, which was at the time the most complete study of the subject ever

5. Ibid.
6. https://articles.mercola.com/sites/articles/archive/2017/12/16/how-much-do-you-know-about-vaccine-safety.aspx

done. It concluded that while the vaccine could cause a fever that triggered a seizure, 'these do not appear to be associated with any long-term adverse consequences'.[7]

To put it another way, all these studies found the idea that the DTP vaccine could cause permanent mental degradation in a child was fake news. This did not stop the anti-vax movement, though, which would soon return to its birthplace – the UK.

In 1998, Britain was once again at the heart of a major anti-vax moment. Dr Andrew Wakefield published research in the prestigious medical journal the *Lancet* that linked the combined vaccination for measles, mumps and rubella (MMR) to autism. The story gathered huge momentum and even the prime minister at the time, Tony Blair, was asked repeatedly if his son Leo had received the vaccination.

As with DTP, newspapers hyped up the MMR risk. The *Daily Mail* ran highly emotive headlines such as 'MMR Killed My Daughter', 'MMR Fears Gain Support', 'New Evidence "Shows MMR Link to Autism"', 'MMR Safe? Baloney. This Is One Scandal That's Getting Worse', 'Scientists Fear MMR Link to Autism' and 'Why I Wouldn't Give My Baby the MMR Jab'.

The *Sun*, the *Express*, the *Telegraph* all piled in with similarly dramatic reporting, but it was not just press deemed to be on the right that were at fault. In 2007, whilst Wakefield was being hauled up in front of the General Medical Council, the *Observer* ran a major interview with him under the headline 'New Health Fears over Big Surge in Autism'. That was a whole three years after journalist Brian Deer had exposed the flaws in Wakefield's work. As recently as 2013 the *Independent* came under fire after it ran a front-page headline: 'MMR Scare

7. Paul A. Offit, *Deadly Choices* (Basic Books, 2010), p. 32.

Doctor: This Outbreak Proves I Was Right'. Its editor at the time, Chris Blackhurst, had to clarify that his paper did not support Wakefield.

In 2004 investigative reporter Brian Deer had cut through the fake news to get to the truth. In the *Sunday Times*, he revealed that Wakefield 'did not disclose he was being funded through solicitors seeking evidence to use against vaccine manufacturers'.

As well as the major conflict of interest, Deer reported: 'The research paper published in the *Lancet* contained no scientific evidence of a link with MMR, only the "association" made by parents. But at the unprecedented press conference to launch the report, attacked the three-in-one jab as posing risks of causing autism and bowel problems.'[8]

Then, as the Wellcome Trust explains: 'In 2010 the study was retracted by its publisher, the *Lancet*, after an investigation discovered multiple conflicts of interest and manipulation of research data.'[9]

There can surely be little doubt that Wakefield published fake news that matches the definition outlined at the beginning of this book. There was incentive for him to find evidence that suited those funding him and publish research that did not have any scientific merit. The consequences were vast.

Not surprisingly given the scare, the numbers of parents giving their children the vaccine dropped considerably. In 1995–6, 91.8 per cent of children received the first jab by their second birthday. By 2003–4, that number had plummeted so that less than 80 per cent of children were vaccinated. It took until 2011 for that number to return to 91.2 per cent.[10]

8. https://briandeer.com/mmr/lancet-deer-1.htm
9. https://wellcomecollection.org/articles/Whf_BSkAACsAgwil
10. https://www.telegraph.co.uk/news/health/news/9705374/MMR-uptake-rates-finally-recovered-from-Wakefield-scandal-figures-show.html

Even banning Wakefield from practising medicine in the UK did not stop him. In 2016 he put out an anti-vax documentary called *Vaxxed*. It reiterated much of his discredited research and was eventually banned from the Tribeca Film Festival in the wake of protests.

However, as a result of his fake news, there have been outbreaks of measles years after he published his bogus theories. Following a record low of cases in 2016, in February 2018 the World Health Organisation (WHO) said there had been a fourfold increase of measles cases across Europe during 2017. This included 35 people dying as a result of the illness.

In June 2018 teenagers, who were at the normal vaccination age when MMR take-up collapsed, were urged to get it, particularly if they were travelling abroad. Commenting at the time, Dr Mary Ramsay, head of immunisation at Public Health England (PHE), warned: 'In the early 2000s there was a fall in MMR vaccination coverage in children and as a consequence we are now seeing measles cases in young adults.'[11] A month later, English health officials were forced to call a 'national measles incident' after PHE recorded 643 cases of measles in the first five and a half months of the year, a sharp rise from the 274 cases the year before.

Those who spread fake news can be the cause of the most devastating consequences. How do we go about tackling this situation?

11. https://www.telegraph.co.uk/science/2018/06/20/teens-missed-mmr-jab-wakefield-scare-urged-seek-vaccination/

PART IV

How do we fix this?

11

Media literacy, transparency and
finding a solution

Much of this book has been devoted to the technological issues
that help fake news spread and the political and social crises
with which they have combined to bring about the post-truth
era.

It should be quite apparent that we cannot allow such a
situation to continue unchallenged. A disregard for the truth
by both citizens and those in power diminishes political
debates, degrades decision-making and damages society at
large. Fake news has put people's lives at risk.

So how can we fight back and reclaim the truth?

The established media, politicians and a host of other
institutions are finding it nearly impossible to do so. As we
have seen, while they may well be sharing proven facts and
reliable information, all too few people are listening. Their
authority has been shot down by scandal and smugness under
a hail of fire from technology-fuelled opponents. Their voices

are now drowned out by many others all presenting information in the same way.

This has not stopped some of those institutions from trying to fix the problem, though. In January 2018, the British government announced it was launching a unit within its intelligence agencies to fight fake news, saying that it would 'respond with more and better use of national security communications to tackle these interconnected complex challenges'.[1]

If nothing else, bringing in the security services demonstrates quite how serious a problem the government considers fake news to be.

The House of Commons Digital, Culture, Media and Sport Committee launched its own inquiry into the problem of fake news that same year. MPs who were members of the committee even travelled to Silicon Valley to interview executives from the major social media firms. The committee's chair, Conservative MP Damian Collins, warned those firms that a failure to get their own houses in order would result in sanction.

Although his committee does not itself have the power to implement anything, Collins said that he wanted to see the implementation of 'some mechanism of saying: if you fail to do that, if you ignore requests to act, if you fail to police the site effectively and deal with highly problematic content, then there has to be some sort of sanction against you'.[2]

However, for many of the reasons highlighted in this book, it hardly seems that politicians are best placed to lead efforts to

1. http://www.bbc.co.uk/news/uk-politics-42791218
2. https://www.theguardian.com/technology/2018/feb/07/commons-committee-must-not-use-term-fake-news-in-us-hearing

tackle fake news – although with consequences as serious as those outlined, it is no wonder they feel compelled to try.

If politicians are going to have any success, they need to make systematic reforms to rebuild trust, not simply demand authority and reverence and expect it to come, as it has in the past. That means not just succumbing to petulant populism and telling people what they want to hear, but doing serious, even inspiring, policy work.

Policies – even those that do not seem immediately connected, such as helping young people get on the housing ladder – policies that create a thriving economy in which wages rise so people can keep up with the cost of living – can do so much to realign people with mainstream politics. More broadly, those advocating centrist, liberal ideas must use such policies to demonstrate that their kind of politics can work to the benefit of the vast majority of people. This will go some way to taking the wind out of the sails of the fake-news-peddling extremists on left and right.

Increased transparency is also crucial. Organisations of all types and at all levels must get far better at showing their working. They need to explain why they make the decisions they do in a far more open and compelling manner than they presently use. If more steps like this are not taken, the information void will continue to be filled by falsehood.

Facebook has moved, albeit slowly, in that direction. Political adverts were a hugely contentious issue across a number of campaigns. It wasn't clear who was paying for a message to be sent to thousands, possibly millions, of people. So, in May 2018 it launched an accessible archive of political adverts. In March 2019 it expanded this, launching a searchable library of all live adverts. Ahead of the EU elections, it also introduced labelling of political adverts across the whole of the

EU, something that had previously only been available in the UK.[3]

Professor Charlie Beckett rightly points out that, for journalists, accountability now has 'a wider sense of not just getting your facts right but being transparent, for example showing your sources, offering opportunities for people to respond and so on'.

Journalism needs to be more of a two-way process, and Tim Dawson gives one simple but potentially effective example of how this can be done, suggesting: 'If you write something up and you've recorded an interview, why not put all of your interviews recorded onto soundcloud?'

Back in 2011 the *Guardian* conducted an experiment with publishing its daily news list online. Such documents are normally closely guarded by editors. Launching the week-long project, then national news editor Dan Roberts said: 'In a world where many readers have been left deeply cynical about journalism after this summer's phone-hacking revelations, it seems there are more people wanting to know where their news comes from and how it is made.'[4]

It is fair to say, in the seven years since he wrote that, the kind of transparency being tested by Roberts and his colleagues has not caught on – not even at the *Guardian* any more.

In the case of the BBC, its head of live political programmes Rob Burley says that in many ways his organisation needs to continue doing what it has been, focussing on impartiality and ignoring outside pressures. However, he does concede that 'we have to explain ourselves better.' He urges colleagues to follow the path he has taken on Twitter and 'push back'. He wants the

3. https://www.macobserver.com/news/facebook-launches-library-of-all-active-adverts/
4. https://www.theguardian.com/help/insideguardian/2011/oct/10/guardian-newslist

BBC to strike a balance: be transparent and show its working, but also be prepared to defend itself.

Another way mainstream outlets are looking to set themselves apart from those publishing fake news is by launching fact-checking services, making themselves the authorities on the truth once again. Over recent years a number of blogs and broadcasts in this vein have emerged in the UK and the US, both from mainstream outlets and from start-ups who sense a gap in the market and ironically look to capitalise on the lack of trust towards existing outlets.

In the UK, the BBC runs the Reality Check website, and Channel 4 has the FactCheck website. While they existed before the outcry about fake news, they have certainly helped establish these major media brands as self-proclaimed arbiters of the truth. In America, outlets like Snopes, PolitiFact and Factcheck.org do similar things.

Their intentions are highly admirable, but plenty of people are happy to dismiss their findings if they do not sit with their preconceptions and ideology. Ultimately, human bias can override whatever data fact-check services can present. After all, if you are convinced there is a conspiracy, why would you not believe the so-called fact checkers are part of it?

Political, government and other public bodies also need to rebuild trust. They could do worse than adopt the principle of transparency along the lines suggested for journalists. They have improved at it to some degree, for instance with more and more data around services being made public. However, this does not tackle the underlying issue of trust. To make progress, those in politics and government need to go beyond the mechanical and make people feel better connected to politics. The default way of doing this in the current age has been to turn to populist figures. They only make the problem worse. We must demand better.

We also need to be clear that not everything is so doom and gloom. As James McGrory told me, he believes that more people than ever before are engaged in politics. He has been working in politics for over decade, but he senses that 'the appetite for debate, for political discussion, for political activism' is the highest it's ever been. 'I run an organisation now that's got half a million people signed up and they want to get out on the streets and campaign. I've never known engagement like it.'

Practitioners in politics and the media can do a lot to restore balance, but it will all be for nothing unless the hugely powerful platforms take action too. Facebook boss Mark Zuckerberg seemed to appreciate this, writing at the start of 2018 that his focus for the year was 'protecting our community from abuse and hate, defending against interference by nation states, or making sure that time spent on Facebook is time well spent'.

The problem is Zuckerberg said something similar at the end of 2016, writing: 'The bottom line is: we take misinformation seriously. Our goal is to connect people with the stories they find most meaningful, and we know people want accurate information.'[5]

As 2018 came to an end, Facebook had once again made some progress, for example introducing more transparency in political adverts on the network by making people publish who has paid for them, but there is still an awful long way to go.

Twitter, too, is struggling to improve matters. It declared in December 2018 that it was 'working hard to detect spammy

5. https://www.facebook.com/zuck/posts/10103269806149061

behaviours at source',[6] but the work of Samantha Bradshaw and colleagues shows how hard that is.

If Facebook and Twitter find it hard to tackle fake news, smaller and more freeform online communities such as 4chan and Reddit find it impossible.

Quite clearly, a problem that has numerous, complex roots requires a wide-ranging response. There are some specific areas that could begin to help turn the tide.

MEDIA LITERACY

One of the key reasons fake news spreads so successfully is a lack of media literacy amongst the general public. People do not understand, because they are not taught, how news comes about, nor how to analyse the information they get. Fixing this is crucial to empowering citizens and stopping fake news from finding footholds so easily.

Media literacy is defined by the Centre for Media Literacy as '[providing] a framework to access, analyse, evaluate, create and participate with messages in a variety of forms'.[7] In other words, it is a way of trying to understand whatever media you are consuming, in whatever form that media comes.

It is often seen as something of a silver bullet for combatting fake news. CNN's senior media correspondent Brian Stelter is one high-profile advocate. Appearing on Recode's *Too Embarrassed to Ask* podcast in February 2017, he bemoaned the fact that 'there are not many media literacy classes in this country. There are not many students being taught media literacy.'

He felt that this was important in 'helping people understand

6. https://blog.twitter.com/official/en_us/topics/company/2017/Our-Approach-Bots-Misinformation.html
7. https://www.medialit.org/media-literacy-definition-and-more

or be able to root out the difference between a credible source and a crazy source' and speculated that the likes of Facebook and Google were interested in funding such work.[8]

It is not difficult to see why improving media literacy is crucial to solving many of the problems outlined over the previous pages. It is objectively hard to argue against the idea that we should all be taught how to better analyse the information we are presented with.

There can be little doubt that some of the issues around fake news have arisen as a result of a failure to critically assess information. Is it likely that the pope would break with centuries of tradition to endorse Donald Trump? Probably not. Is it really likely that Hillary Clinton is running a paedophile ring from the basement of a Washington pizza parlour? No, it is not. All too often, though, people see a random headline and take it at face value. They are unequipped with the tools to critically evaluate whether it is from a 'credible source or a crazy source', to use Stelter's phrase.

It may have new advocates, but the push for media literacy is not entirely new. LSE social psychology professor Sonia Livingstone and fellow academic Yinhan Wang wrote in 2011 that 'the media landscape that the public must navigate grows more complex daily. The risks of consumer detriment and digital/social exclusion are also growing.' They identified the key issue back then and argued that media literacy should be promoted to benefit 'the whole population... disadvantaged populations... the state... citizens'.[9]

However, as Livingstone explained in a later work, this is

8. https://www.recode.net/2017/2/8/14542732/full-transcript-cnn-senior-media-correspondent-brian-stelter-fake-news
9. Sonia Livingstone and Yinhan Wang, *Media Literacy and the Communications Act: What Has Been Achieved and What Should Be Done?* A 2013 update, http://eprints.lse.ac.uk/56431/1/LSEMPPBrief2_2013Update.pdf.

rather more difficult in practice than in theory. 'What media literacy includes is a moving target,' she wrote for the LSE's Media Policy Project in 2018. 'We cannot teach everyone all they need to know.' Livingstone also conceded that 'media education is a long-term solution' and so it cannot quickly reverse the trends we have seen rear their ugly head in recent years.

That does not mean that increased media literacy does not have its place. And sometimes the positive impact can happen more quickly than we might imagine. Teacher Scott Bedley recounted on Vox.com how he taught his 10- and 11-year-old students to fact-check things and identify fake news, using a variety of techniques. (The initiative came after a student had embarrassed himself in front of his classmates by sharing some false information he had found via Google.)

Bedley says that he told his students to ask themselves seven questions when looking at a piece of news:

- Copyright: Who, if anyone, is claiming ownership of the information?

- Verification with multiple sources: Double check the information on multiple websites.

- Credibility of source: Check if the source has been recently created, as sites that have been around for longer can demonstrate their reliability over time; newer sources do not have that track record.

- Date published: Check how recently the webpage was updated to see how up to date it is.

- Author's expertise: Does the author have expertise in and a long, serious history with the subject?

- Does it match your prior knowledge: Does the information correlate with what we already know?

- Does it seem realistic: This comes down to common sense – is what we are being told realistic?

Bedley says that when he gave his children these questions and made them practise running through the list on news articles, they quickly grasped the concept. 'One unintended consequence is that I now have 33 10-year-old fact checkers in my classroom that I've empowered to call me out if I'm sharing fake news,' he writes.[10]

Yes, children famously pick things up more quickly than adults, but this shows that media literacy is far from academic. It is essential that we improve our media literacy if we are ever going to combat the surge of fake news.

LESS IS MORE

Give that part of the problem is a lack of trust in mainstream media, it is down to the media itself to improve, to maintain its value to consumers and cut through the fake news. Instead, we the public are inundated with repeats of the same information.

Professor Beckett says: 'If you pick up most newspapers, they've got, broadly speaking, very similar stories. In the past that didn't matter because you were a *Guardian* reader. But if it's all mixed up online, then you'll go with the best take,' and 'the BBC will keep you updated with general news. So where are they adding value?'

If all the newspapers are telling one story, but another website is writing about something different, then that is more

10. https://www.vox.com/first-person/2017/3/29/15042692/fake-news-education-election

interesting to readers. It may be true, it may be false, but that will be hard to distinguish.

Beckett says that 'it's only in the last year or two [the mainstream media have] really woken up to this. And they are all doing fewer stories and they are trying to do them deeper and better and differently and they're shifting their agenda.'

He does think they are responding not least because 'they realise it's a business-model problem. If they are not seen as purveyors of truthful stuff, if they're not seen as relevant, people are not going to pay attention to them and therefore they are not going to make any money.'

In recent times some media entrepreneurs have tried to use this approach to gain popularity. One notable example is Tortoise Media, founded by former BBC news chief and *Times* editor James Harding and set to launch in 2019. He described the outlet to the BBC's media editor, Amol Rajan, as 'the love-child of TED Talks and the *Economist*'.

Operating under the banner 'Slow down, wise up', Harding and his team want to cut out the excess noise and bring their readers closer to the news-making process by hosting daily meetings which members can attend. It is certainly worth trying, and the intention of slowing down the news is a worthy one, but I think it risks being rather exclusive. The type of people who are able to attend such events are likely to be well off and time rich. It is hardly going to be taking people out of their bubbles. Indeed, it risks doing little more than taking the current echo chamber offline.[11]

What Harding has rightly identified, though, is that media needs to slow down. It needs to help people navigate the information overload we are suffering from, not add to it. There are so many interesting, compelling, in-depth ways of

---

11. https://www.bbc.co.uk/news/entertainment-arts-45875284

telling a story now that there is no need for media outlets to simply churn things out. The fakers do that.

We are never going to go back to an age in which people just read one newspaper once a day and then maybe catch up via an evening news bulletin. Frankly, we wouldn't want to. But if credible news organisations slow down a bit, offering something other than the churn, they will have more value to customers, who will then go to them instead of to less credible outlets.

12

Conclusion

Looking into the post-truth era can be a rather dispiriting experience. We have undergone a profound, technology-powered shift in our political, social and media lives that has empowered lies and liars. It is not clear how, or whether, the pendulum can ever swing back in the direction of truth.

It must do, though. We cannot continue to operate in the toxic atmosphere of anger and untruths that has already cost people their lives and will doubtlessly do so again. Whether we are executives at a tech giant, newspaper editors or ordinary citizens reading the news, all of us must take a long, hard look at ourselves and ask how we can improve things.

Politicians in the liberal centre need to find the energy and ideas to counter the extremists on left and right and bring politics back to a more reasonable place. We do not all have to agree, and we do not have to turn our backs on radicalism, but a return to some norms would be no bad thing. Fake news thrives on political polarisation.

For most of us, this means calling out the politicians who

take us for fools by repeating lies. It means sometimes having uncomfortable conversations with friends and family when they share things online that we know are not accurate. It means not rewarding publications that publish fake news with clicks.

Any progress could become redundant as America hurtles towards the 2020 presidential election. After years of lying to New York tabloids, Donald Trump came to power as America's forty-fifth president, thanks to fake news. He is unlikely to give up on the tactic that has worked so well for him. His opponents must not sink to his level, but instead come up with far better tactics for combatting Trump's fake news.

The fallout from Brexit, too, will require raising the tone of debate, not sinking to the low levels we saw during the campaign. Unfortunately, that does not seem very likely either. As discussed earlier in this book, politicians and campaigners alike succumbed to the most vicious, violent language as the exit negotiations process reached its climax.

For all concerned, perhaps the most pertinent question of all, the one that really sums up the dilemma of the post-truth era, comes from the BBC's Rob Burley: 'Ultimately, what can we do but present the truth?'

Acknowledgements

There are a number of people I'd like to thank who have played significant roles in helping me get this book done. First and foremost, my family – my mum, Sue, my dad, Paul, sisters Gemma and Sarah, and brother-in-law James. Your support, guidance and patience the whole way through has been invaluable. I could not have done it without you. I am also immensely grateful for the love of my grandparents, Jacqueline and Gerald, and that of my aunts, uncles and cousins with whom I am lucky to share such a close relationship.

My friends, too, have been amazingly supportive in this process by making me laugh when I needed it, tolerating my whining, or simply buying me a drink and telling me it was going to be OK. You know who you are and how much you mean to me.

I'd also like to thank the team at Unbound, who believed in this book from the start. Firstly, Katy, who brought me into Unbound, having previously commissioned me for the *Independent on Sunday*. Some people turn up and help you kick-on at key points of your life and career. Katy is one such person for me. Jessica, Xander, Georgia, Josephine, Sara have all been fantastically supportive at each different stage too. Writing a book has always been a dream of mine, and you all helped turn that dream into a reality.

Of course, given the nature of Unbound, I couldn't have done this without the pledgers – the people who bought this book before it even existed. I hope you are all proud of the finished product that features your name.

Unbound is the world's first crowdfunding publisher, established in 2011.

We believe that wonderful things can happen when you clear a path for people who share a passion. That's why we've built a platform that brings together readers and authors to crowdfund books they believe in – and give fresh ideas that don't fit the traditional mould the chance they deserve.

This book is in your hands because readers made it possible. Everyone who pledged their support is listed at the front of the book and below. Join them by visiting unbound.com and supporting a book today.

Joe Otten
Kiki Rayne
Danny Rothberg
Gerard Scott
Andy Silvester
Rich and Sarah Smith
Monika Smrj

Alex Sword
Stephen Tall
Danny Temko
Adam Tinworth
David Zaharik
Kieran Zucker